PATIENTS

VIEW THEIR

PSYCHOTHERAPY

PATIENTS

VIEW THEIR

PSYCHOTHERAPY

HANS H. STRUPP

RONALD E. FOX

KEN LESSLER

THE JOHNS HOPKINS PRESS, BALTIMORE AND LONDON

The Johns Hopkins Press, Baltimore, Maryland 21218
The Johns Hopkins Press Ltd., London

Library of Congress Catalog Card Number 75-85341

Standard Book Number 8018-1053-1

To the memory of
Martin S. Wallach,
collaborator and friend

CONTENTS

Figures

Appendix Figures

Tables

Appendix Tables

FOREWORD

The field of psychotherapy, after several decades of research, still suffers from a dearth of hard facts. Since there is no solid basis for choosing between different forms of psychotherapy, new methods proliferate and all persist. In the United States today psychoanalysis in all its guises, client-centered therapy, hypnotherapies, behavior therapies, implosion therapy, and a host of group and family therapies all claim successes.

Most researchers, struggling toward solid ground in this morass, have selected questions for study on the basis of amenability to statistical measurement and control, rather than relevance, so that their results decrease in significance as they increase in precision and reliability. The studies of Dr. Strupp and his colleagues may be counted among the exceptions to this rule. He has never succumbed to the whims of fashion but has consistently focused on the psychotherapeutic method which is, in actuality, dominant in America—self-exploration under the guidance of an expert who offers acceptance and understanding, its goal

increased autonomy and personal growth. His basic assumption has been that it is premature to design experiments to test specific hypotheses about psychotherapy
until there is a clearer understanding of the relationship of
the interaction of patient and therapist to the outcome of
treatment. The approach to this multifaceted question, he
feels, must be empirical rather than experimental, relying
on systematic observations of the processes and outcome of
actual treatment, based on retrospective reports from
patients obtained through a searching questionnaire and
through the initial evaluations, progress notes, and case
summaries in the clinic records.

Researchers have long looked askance at such data. At
first, influenced by psychoanalysis, they assumed that the
truly important features of the human psyche are buried
in the Unconscious and that the feelings and thoughts of
which a person is aware and can report are therefore necessarily superficial. Patients' subjective reports then came under attack by the behavior therapists, who maintained that
the only valid evidence of the effects of therapy was objec-
tively measurable behavior.

Patients' retrospective reports are indeed subject to distortions created both by the circumstances in which they
are obtained and by the falsifications of memory, but, as
this study demonstrates, they can yield important information. Similarly, researchers have been inclined to underestimate the information that can be gleaned from clinic
records because they are prepared by busy practitioners
and are inevitably spotty and incomplete. Here, too, they
have thrown the baby out with the bath water, for when
systematically analyzed, such records often provide much
useful information. Moreover, for the researcher retrospective reports and routine clinic records have an advan-

tage that must not be overlooked: they do not introduce distortions into the psychotherapeutic process by the very act of studying it. Nobody knows the magnitude and nature of the effect produced on therapist and patient by the necessity of filling out special records repeatedly during the course of therapy or of having researchers looking over their shoulders.

Like all of the work of Dr. Strupp and his associates, this study is characterized by diligent, careful accumulation and thorough analysis of the data. The rarest of its virtues is that it replicates their previous findings. The authors state their position clearly and convincingly and evaluate its strengths and limitations dispassionately, with a mature, balanced perspective. *Patients View Their Psychotherapy* is a model of naturalistic research in psychotherapy, and the richness of the findings presented here bears witness to the continuing value of this temporarily unfashionable approach.

JEROME D. FRANK, M.D.
Professor of Psychiatry
The Johns Hopkins University School of Medicine

PREFACE

Every scientific discipline can profit from periodic re-examination of the empirical data on which its theories and generalizations are based. In a discipline as complex, young, and essentially undeveloped as psychotherapy, such an endeavor seems particularly appropriate. In this book we set ourselves the task of studying what former psychotherapy patients said about the nature of their emotional problems and what seemed to have helped them. More specifically, we were interested in exploring the reasons they gave for seeking the help of a psychotherapist, the steps they took to become patients, the experiences they underwent during therapy, and their reactions to the experience. We asked the patients to speak for themselves and to assess the over-all value of their experience.

Modern psychotherapy generally traces its beginning to the pioneering work of Freud around the turn of the century. It is a tribute to his ingenuity that he was able to discern in the accounts of his patients a meaning, continuity, and logic which had escaped the attention of his predecessors. To a considerable extent the last fifty years have been devoted to the verification and elaboration of Freud's original hypotheses.

New observations tend to confirm old ones, and it is difficult to view phenomena from new vantage points. Psychotherapists still listen to patients, of course, but what they hear is heavily influenced by their expectations. The very magnitude of Freud's discoveries may have blinded later investigators to alternative formulations which may be equally cogent and persuasive. Theorists who rely upon non-Freudian assumptions fare no better; they too must fit empirical data into their theoretical frameworks. One need not belabor the point that the phenomena do not speak for themselves but are subject to the observer's interpretations and constructions.

In studying these patients' reports, we sought to preserve the phenomenological nature of their experiences so that new trends or different emphases could emerge. Our work proceeded on the assumption that subjective data, while certainly fallible, nevertheless represent an important source of information. Moreover, we did not confine ourselves to the reports but complemented them with what were presumed to be more objective data from external sources— clinical charts, therapists' reports, and the like. There is reason to believe that the patients whose experiences are described here are a fairly representative sample of the kinds of people who apply for professional psychotherapeutic help throughout the country.

Our objective, however, went beyond recording the experiences of one group of patients, useful though such information may be. We were interested in the broader question of the value and promise of outpatient psychotherapy.

What does it have to offer? Can we predict the kinds of outpatients whose therapy will be successful? Does length of therapy have any bearing on outcome? What kinds of personality changes may reasonably be expected from this form of therapy? What are the patients' perceptions of the therapist and the therapeutic relationship?

The present gap between the number of people needing help and the professional manpower available to provide it will become greater in the next few years. Hence our manpower resources must be conserved and the efficiency of the services now rendered increased. At the same time, however, we are convinced that in the long run refinements in therapeutic methods will come from systematic research designed to advance the knowledge of psychological processes upon which psychotherapy ultimately rests. It is our hope that the research reported in these pages will form a building block in this endeavor.

The empirical data presented derived from two questionnaire surveys of former patients. Private patients who had been seen in individual psychotherapy by psychotherapists (principally psychiatrists) over an extended period made up the first survey group. The second, a larger sample of clinic patients, was included to broaden our investigative efforts. Both groups of patients were asked to respond to what was virtually the same questionnaire, and the analysis of the data was handled in a comparable way. Both studies were carried out in the Department of Psychiatry of the University of North Carolina, and all therapists were members of its professional staff. Hence, despite certain procedural differences, the studies are closely related. Furthermore, the experience gained by the research staff in the first study greatly facilitated the subsequent work. Both investigations are part of a larger program of research in psychotherapy.

A word should be said about the organization of this book. In Chapter 1 the stage is set and the broader issues and research problems with which we were concerned are discussed. In Chapter 2 we provide a summary of the research findings of the first study, which is based on an earlier published report (Strupp, Wallach, and Wogan 1964; the reader interested in the design, execution, and conclusions of the earlier study may wish to consult this source). Chapter 3 presents selected case histories based upon the raw material collected in the course of both studies. Since the two patient samples did not seem to differ in any substantive way, no distinction was made between case histories chosen from Study 1 and from Study 2. In Chapters 4 through 7 we report in detail Study 2, which in major respects was patterned on the first investigation. Technical material—research instruments, instructions, procedural details, and steps in the statistical analyses—is included in the Appendixes, to which reference is made in the text where appropriate. In Chapters 8 and 9 we have attempted to synthesize our research findings and to discuss their general implications. The reader who wishes to obtain a quick overview may want to consult Chapters 1, 2, 3, 8, and 9.

ACKNOWLEDGMENTS

The first study reported here was supported in part by Research Grant MH 02171 from the U.S. Public Health Service National Institute of Mental Health. It was reported in H. H. Strupp, M. S. Wallach, and M. Wogan, Psychotherapy experience in retrospect: questionnaire survey of former patients and their therapists, *Psychological Monographs* 78 (1964). The second study and the preparation of the manuscript were aided by faculty grants from the School of Medicine of the University of North Carolina and from Vanderbilt University. Thomas E. Curtis, M.D., Director of the Psychiatric Outpatient Clinic at the University of North Carolina, was most helpful in our research. Professor Lyle V. Jones contributed valuable statistical advice, and the Department of Biostatistics at the University of North Carolina was most generous in providing consultation and computer services.

We wish to thank the therapists who participated in the first study for enlisting the patients' interest and cooperation and for the ratings they made available to our research staff. The dedication and interest of our research assistant, Mrs. Patricia Vandiviere, who worked with the project from its inception, made her a collaborator and a friend on whom we could always rely. We are grateful to Mrs. Jean Owen, of The Johns Hopkins Press, whose editorial help greatly improved the style of our work. Our greatest debt, of course, is to the patients whose diligence and frankness in providing the data made the book possible. They are anonymous, and their help can be only inadequately acknowledged in this way.

Dr. Martin S. Wallach, a key member of our research team and co-author of the first study, did not live to see the completion of the book in which he was so deeply invested. As a small token of our friendship, this volume is dedicated to his memory.

PATIENTS

VIEW THEIR

PSYCHOTHERAPY

I believe that psychoanalysts, in listening to life-histories for more than half a century, have developed an "unofficial" image of the strengths inherent in the individual life cycle and in the sequence of generations. I think here of those most enjoyable occasions when we can agree that a patient has really improved—not, as the questionnaires try to make us say, markedly improved, or partially improved—but essentially so. Here, the loss of symptoms is mentioned only in passing, while the decisive criterion is an increase in the strength and staying power of the patient's concentration on pursuits which are somehow right, whether it is in love or in work, in home life, friendship, or citizenship.

ERIK ERIKSON

1.

INTRODUCTION

Is it effective? What changes does it produce? How does it work? How long does it take? Whenever psychotherapy (and psychoanalysis, as one of its variants) is the topic of discussion, these questions arise. They have been asked by the public, patients, therapists, and researchers ever since psychotherapy emerged as a professional specialty around the turn of the century. Former patients who feel they have been helped and psychotherapists who have strong commitments to their profession require no demonstrations from a scientific investigator, while members of the medical profession frequently view psychotherapy with awe, disdain, or doubt, and use referral to a psychiatrist as a last resort when they are confronted with a patient whom they find troublesome and whose difficulties are apparently "emotional."

The din of controversy has made it exceedingly difficult for the interested layman to have an informed opinion. Some individuals have deep-seated prejudices against an enterprise which they place on a par with faith healing, religious conversion, "do-goodism," quackery, or worse.

They seize avidly on research reports questioning the effectiveness of psychotherapy to confirm these preconceptions. Another large segment of the public simply wants to know what psychotherapy has to offer. Whether or not they have read Freud, they sense that psychotherapy is quite unlike any other "treatment": they are familiar with the psychoanalyst of the cartoons who appears to spend his life sitting behind a patient on a couch scribbling free associations on a note pad, and they are curious.

Gradually the view is gaining acceptance that psychotherapy is not a form of medical treatment and that analogies to medicine are grossly misleading. Modern psychotherapy grew out of medicine, and the great innovators like Freud, Adler, Jung, Harry Stack Sullivan, and others were usually physicians. This heritage accounts for such terms as "patient," "doctor," "psychopathology," "treatment," and "cure," which are still widely used but are almost certainly destined for obsolescence. However, psychotherapy involves a set of psychological techniques for influencing another person, and, to the extent that analogies are helpful, it resembles education much more closely than medical treatment.

The therapist teaches and the patient learns. As a teacher, the therapist is an expert; the patient is a student. The therapist also functions as a parent in the eyes of the patient, who unwittingly assumes the role of a child and casts the therapist in that role. As a teacher (or substitute parent), he dispenses rewards and punishments and employs a variety of psychological techniques for helping the patient achieve greater autonomy and self-direction (Szasz 1965). The goals of psychotherapy are independence, maturity, and adulthood. Accordingly, what ails the patient is not a disease: the "symptoms" of which he complains and which impel him to seek help are part and parcel of his personal immaturity. Basically, he wants to be a child and uses infantile techniques to attain a mixture of infantile and adult goals. His dilemma is that he as well as society finds his immaturity and his stratagems unacceptable; he deceives himself, and yet he is often outraged by his dimly perceived childishness. This is neurosis, pure and simple. Persons suffering from so-called personality disorders, behavior disorders, or character disorders essentially fit this description, although their conflicts and "symptoms" may not be apparent.

Various theories of psychopathology and neurosis have been put forth to explain how the patient became the kind of person that he is. They are of theoretical interest and potential preventive value. But as far as his work with the patient is concerned, they are of no immediate concern to the therapist. The patient learned to become the person that he is, and all that the therapist can do is help him learn different ways of feeling and behaving. He can enlighten him (through "interpretations") about patterns of behavior which have been and are still maladaptive, that is, which interfere with his adult goals. Once he has deeply experienced and recognized the error or foolishness of his ways ("insight"), he may gradually modify his behavior. On the other hand, the therapist, through more direct means, such as suggestion, counterconditioning, etc., may influence the patient's attitudes and behavior. If he employs the former approach, he must have the patient's interest and cooperation. The patient's motivation is crucial and further distinguishes him from the medical patient, whose cooperation rarely extends beyond taking the prescribed medicine at specified times or adhering to some other regimen.

Psychotherapy calls for almost total commitment on the patient's part. The problem facing the therapist is that, the patient's avowed willingness to cooperate notwithstanding, he also has a large investment in maintaining the status quo ("resistance"). Overcoming this resistance is a large part of the therapeutic effort and requires a considerable amount of perspicacity and technical skill. Analytically oriented or "dynamic" therapists in the tradition of Freud, who use this indirect approach, assert that the hard work expended by the patient in combating his devious, self-defeating ("neurotic") tendencies results in the acquisition of strength, tolerance of frustration, and the toughness that grows out of the realization that infantile wishes and goals cannot be fulfilled (Menninger 1958). This painful process of growing up, of becoming an adult, is what such therapists mean by "reconstructive efforts" or "restructuring the personality." This form of psychotherapy can never be a pleasant experience; as a matter of fact, it always entails hard work and further suffering.

From this summary it should be apparent that the analytically oriented therapist is not primarily interested in "symptom relief" or "symptom removal." While he realizes that any neurotic symptom means (among other things) that the patient is suffering, and he is dedicated to the alleviation of human suffering, he views symptoms as a manifestation of a faulty approach to the solution of life's problems. His working assumption is that once the patient has achieved greater maturity and autonomy his symptoms will diminish or disappear. In contrast, therapists whose aim is the direct modification of behavior through such techniques as counterconditioning, desensitization, and the like (Eysenck 1959; Wolpe 1958; Wolpe and Lazarus 1966) are, for the most part, not concerned with the patient's motivation to seek change, nor do they view neurotic symptoms as indications of a faulty life style. Their view is that the symptom *is* the neurosis and that the removal of the symptom will enable the patient to bring into play adult skills and strengths, which he is assumed to possess to a greater or lesser extent regardless of his neurotic difficulties.

It is essential to point out here that the analytic therapist is fully aware that the patient, while infantile in some respects, is mature and quite capable of managing his life in others. The issue is that of the degree to which neurotic difficulties interfere with his total functioning and cause personal suffering and unhappiness. People who come to a psychiatric clinic or to private practitioners for the most part do not present isolated symptoms in otherwise mature personalities. Their unwitting but persistent clinging to infantile strategies and goals has deprived them of many opportunities for developing the skill in getting along with others which is part of the normal adult's repertoire. In this respect, they are comparable to school dropouts who wish to re-enter school but have missed large portions of the curriculum. Therapeutic learning cannot make up for this deficit. All it can do is reopen doors which seemed closed for good. The patient still faces the arduous task of overcoming his handicaps by greater participation in living, learning by trial and error, and plain hard work.

Yet whatever his goals or theoretical convictions, whether his training has been in medicine and psychiatry or has been non-medical, the *modus operandi* of the psychotherapist is the employment of psychological techniques. Whenever a psychiatrist prescribes one of the psychoactive drugs which relieve anxiety, influence moods, or alleviate other symptoms, he is functioning not as a psychotherapist but as a physician who is concerned with the body as a physiochemical machine, not with learned behavior or motivation. This is not to say that under some circumstances the combination of drugs and psychotherapy may not be beneficial and indeed highly desirable, but the unique role and function of the psychotherapist and of psychotherapy must be understood.

To return to the question of the therapeutic results and effectiveness of psychotherapy, if neurosis and character disorders are not diseases but patterns of learned behavior which psychotherapy is designed to modify, it becomes apparent that terms like "cure," "improvement," and so on, are meaningful only in the most general sense. What constitutes improvement? Who is to be the judge, the patient, the therapist, the patient's family, outside observers? How durable must changes be in order to be considered "improvement"? Would the changes have occurred spontaneously if no psychotherapy had been undertaken? Changes may not be the result of the procedures and skill of the therapist but of the warm, accepting atmosphere created by a "professional friend" (Schofield 1964). Perhaps other procedures, less expensive, time-consuming, and demanding, would achieve comparable results. There are modes of therapy for which extensive training is not as essential as it is for our current methods. These troublesome questions are legitimate subjects for scientific inquiry. Society has a right to expect that professional services which in many states are licensed by law and which are subsidized by the taxpayer in all states, deliver what they promise.

The fact that the effectiveness of psychotherapy has been questioned suggests that its results are far from dramatic; indeed, they are often equivocal and even unknown. The utility of a drug like penicillin is fairly easily established, and even when the precise nature of its pharmacological action is unknown (as in the case of aspirin), the pragmatic evidence of its effectiveness is sufficient. The difficulty in evaluating psychotherapeutic treatment, then, is in establishing the outcome criteria one is willing to accept. Despite extensive research (three major national conferences on psychotherapy have recently been held and are reported in Rubinstein and Parloff 1959; Strupp and Luborsky 1962; and Shlien et al. 1968), general agreement has not been reached. The problems of controlled research in this area are highly complex and technical (for an excellent discussion of them, see Frank 1959), but it may be seen that meaningful comparisons of patients, techniques, and results depend to a large extent upon specification of variables and the situational context.

It is as useful to talk about the effectiveness of psychotherapy in general as to talk about the effectiveness of an appendectomy without specification of the condition which it is intended to remedy. The problem is further complicated by the fact that although an appendectomy consists of a highly specific set of procedures which can be carried out by any qualified surgeon, the same cannot be said of psychotherapy. One investigator (Paul 1966) asked college students who experienced anxiety when speaking in public to volunteer for a treatment program of five sessions designed to alleviate the problem. If at the end of the series the student's anxiety had markedly decreased, he was considered improved. Another group of investigators (Lang and Lazovik 1963) sought out persons who admitted to a fear of snakes and desensitized them to holding a reptile in their hands. A third group of researchers (Bachrach, Erwin, and Mohr 1965), using another technique, recorded a therapeutic success when a hospitalized patient who had chronically refused the intake of food could enter the dining room and feed herself. Other investigators (Rogers and Dymond 1954), working along the more "traditional" lines of client-centered therapy, did psychotherapy of young adults who complained of a variety of neurotic symptoms, and measured their success in terms of a change in the client's self-concept. Finally, analytic treatment centers report under several headings the results of the therapy of patients suffering from a wide variety of symptoms and difficulties.

To be sure, each investigator is at liberty to define his therapeutic goals, which others may consider either "far-reaching" or "trivial"; similarly, each investigator can define "improvement" in any way he likes. What he cannot do, however, as long as there is a sharp divergence in the kinds of outcomes achieved with different techniques, is claim superiority for his particular techniques, nor can he force therapists using techniques of their own choosing to employ them toward other goals. All of these restrictions have been violated to varying degrees by investigators attempting to demonstrate the superiority of one technique over another. Comparisons between patients in therapy and so-called untreated controls have suffered from similar defects (Eysenck 1952, 1961). A fundamental requirement for any scientific experiment is standardization of the experimental situation and the measuring technique. With respect to the problem of outcomes in psychotherapy, it must be concluded that such standardization has not been achieved. The difficulties are not insurmountable, and we may well see approximations to solutions in future. For the time being, however, we are dealing with an open issue.

The patient or prospective patient, of course, is not interested in statistics except insofar as he can apply them to himself. In Chapter 9, therefore, we present some guidelines which we hope may help the reader to form a more realistic picture of what a patient may expect from psychotherapy whether he seeks the services of a therapist in private practice or a mental health clinic. Psychotherapy is no panacea, clinics render service of variable quality, clinic therapists are typically inexperienced, and psychotherapy entails material and personal sacrifices. Further, the reader is warned that there is a certain risk that a patient may feel that his condition is worse after therapy than it was before (for a further documentation of this finding, see Bergin 1963). Nevertheless, the odds are that he will consider his psychotherapy exceedingly beneficial and that through it he will acquire skills which will enable him to deal more effectively with the vicissitudes of a decidedly imperfect society. Whether the gains experienced are purely subjective or demonstrable by objective criteria as well is a question of no interest to

the patient who feels that his suffering has diminished and that the experience has been worth while.

If an individual is beset with the kinds of personal difficulties which are usually amenable to psychotherapy, if his life circumstances are appropriate, and if therapeutic facilities are available, should he embark on a course of individual psychotherapy? Partial answers to these questions are offered in the following chapters, but ultimately this is a highly personal decision, analogous in many ways to the choice of a career. On the basis of his talents, aptitudes, intelligence, and other factors, a person may anticipate success in numerous vocations. He can enlist the help of a vocational counselor and his friends, but he must make the decision in the end. In the same way, the patient's personal commitment to therapy is of over-riding importance. There is ample evidence that patients for whom psychotherapy is "prescribed" by someone else or who for some other reason enter the therapeutic situation involuntarily are poor risks.

For the individual who does decide to seek psychotherapeutic help, society provides many institutions and settings which in a broad sense may be said to provide it. One can join a religious group or become a convert to a faith; one can seek solutions to personal problems through involvement in charitable activities; one can become a member of a multitude of cults; group psychotherapy or individual psychotherapy of a particular variety may seem to have something valuable to offer. Often a person must determine through trial and error what is best for him. This search may be disillusioning, but in the process he is bound to learn something about himself, including his limitations.

Patient and psychotherapist constitute a particular kind of human relationship which, despite its frequent ambiguity in actual practice, is based on the belief that an objective examination of troublesome problems in living, undertaken in the context of a professional relationship over time, can clarify them and increase one's autonomy and mastery of feelings, impulses, and patterns of behavior. Abstract as this approach may sound, it eschews mysterious or esoteric forces. Its emphasis is on rationality, personal autonomy, and self-determination. While the processes of psychological change are far from adequately understood, the psychotherapist's assumption is that persistent work on a problem is more likely than incantations or lamentations to lead to its resolution. In short, meaningful help is in the long run self-help. Admittedly, dynamic psychotherapy demands a great deal from the patient, but if he is fortunate enough to be a "good" patient and to encounter a competent therapist with whom he can work effectively, he may go some distance toward becoming the master of his fate.

2.

THE INITIAL STUDY:
A SUMMARY

The impetus for our initial study of the psychotherapy experience in retrospect came from a desire to gain a better understanding of factors in the patient-therapist relationship which might account for therapeutic change. Using a sample of private patients who had been seen by experienced psychotherapists (in this case principally psychiatrists) over an extended period of time, we addressed ourselves to the following questions: (1) To what extent is a given therapeutic outcome associated with specifiable characteristics of the patient-therapist interaction? (2) What part does the therapist's behavior (personal style, techniques, etc.) play in the outcome of the psychotherapy? Is it possible to identify sets of attitudes to describe the therapeutic atmosphere? (3) To what extent do patients and therapists agree on the quality of their working relationship, their attitudes toward each other, and the results of the treatment? Finally, we were interested in exploring possible relationships between the results of the psychotherapy and such variables as the duration of the treatment, possible differences between "psychotherapy" and "psychoanalysis," and socioenvironmental factors.

A comprehensive questionnaire (see Appendix A) was designed, pretested, and mailed to seventy-six former patients by eleven psychotherapists who had agreed to collaborate with the investigators. In order to obtain parallel evaluations against which the patients' ratings could be compared, each participating therapist completed a series of global ratings on each patient (see Appendix B). The patient sample was equally divided between men and women; ten of the eleven therapists were men.

Completed questionnaires were received from forty-four patients, representing a return rate of 58 per cent.* The question of response bias, which usually arises in studies of this kind, could not be answered conclusively, but there was a suggestion that non-respondents had received more therapy than respondents. Moreover, the therapists' evaluations of therapeutic results tended to be more positive about the respondent group. While most differences were slight, patients rated as successful by their therapists were

* It is important to understand that, although the therapist sent a questionnaire to each patient over his signature, his letter clearly stated that the form was to be returned to the research staff, not to him. Furthermore, the patient could indicate whether he would permit his responses to be shown to his therapist or preferred to remain anonymous. Most respondents were indifferent on this question. It was essential for the patient's former therapist to initiate the contact because of its confidential nature, and his assurances of anonymity may not have completely dispelled the patient's concern about responding frankly. However, we believe that this approach went far toward eliciting candid responses.

In the second study all patients were approached by the director of the North Carolina Memorial Hospital Outpatient Clinic. As in the first study, their completed questionnaires were returned to the research staff. No questionnaire was shown to a therapist unless his patient specified that it might be. All questionnaires, charts, and so on, were assigned code numbers, and, in any case, the research staff had no interest in the identity of individual respondents.

more likely to respond to the questionnaire than those rated as less successful. Of our respondents 70 per cent were married, and 61 per cent of the married group had at least one child. The median age was 31 to 32 years at the beginning of therapy, 35 at the time of the survey. Most patients were fairly well-to-do: the median family income ranged between $7,500 and $10,000 a year. Educational level, too, was high: the median was sixteen years, which placed the sample at the level of college graduates. Professionals made up 28 per cent of the sample, 16 per cent occupied managerial positions, and 27 per cent were housewives. In terms of Hollingshead's Index of Social Position (Hollingshead and Redlich 1958, pp. 37–38), most of the patients belonged to the upper social classes and are thus representative of the clientele of the average therapist in private practice.

The average patient was seen for 166 interviews, and therapy typically lasted 28 months. Interviews were usually scheduled twice a week. The mean number of months since termination was 32. Almost 75 per cent of the patients had only one therapist, but 14 per cent were treated by three or more. While distinctions between psychoanalysis and psychotherapy were difficult to draw, approximately one-third of the respondents were seen in psychoanalysis. The median fee was fifteen dollars an hour (which must be judged rather low by current standards; however, the study was carried out in the early 1960's, and a number of respondents were low-fee patients).

The patients represented the full range of emotional disturbances. The fact that almost one-half of the respondents had a record of previous hospitalizations for psychiatric reasons clearly indicates that this group had problems in living that were neither minor nor transient. This judgment was corroborated both by the patients and their therapists.

Two-thirds to three-quarters of the respondents, depending upon the wording of the question, credited the therapy experience with significant improvements in their personal well-being, and these favorable results were described as lasting. The therapists, while somewhat more cautious in their retrospective evaluations, for the most part agreed with the patients' appraisals. Even more impressive than percentage figures were the patients' reports of the changes they attributed to the experience. These commentaries by non-professional people, paralleling as they did claims made for psychotherapy in the professional literature, were considered extremely valuable evidence of an increased sense of mastery and the achievement of conscious control over impulses, symptoms, and neurotic trends.

The patients' accounts also revealed that the disappearance of specific symptoms was only a minor aspect of the improvement they experienced. Even in the more limited and abbreviated courses of therapy there were gains which approximated the kinds of far-reaching changes experienced by patients in more intensive therapy. It is important to emphasize this point, frequently lost sight of by the proponents of conditioning therapies, which focus largely on the amelioration of specific symptoms. The significant gains emphasized by most of our respondents were increased mastery not only over specific symptoms but in many areas of living. Thus they forcefully called attention to the function of psychotherapy as an educational or re-educational process.

We were further able to demonstrate substantial areas of agreement between patients and therapists concerning the essential aspects and results of the therapeutic experience. Even subjective data are capable of consensual validation in some form. On the assumption that the therapists' evaluations had an objective core, and on the basis of a highly positive correlation coefficient (in the neighborhood of .60), we were able to attribute a measure of objectivity to the patients' assessments as well.

The detailed accounts of each patient (matched by briefer therapists' judgments) provide a rich source of data concerning the manner in which he experienced the therapy, his perceptions of the therapist and his techniques, the nature of the problems which led him to enter therapy, and the character of the changes which he attributed to the therapeutic interaction. Personality changes resulting from psychotherapy have often been described, but very rarely have such accounts come from the patient himself. Despite the imperfections of the measuring instruments, the rather substantial agreement between patients and therapists in their assessment of each other, of the relationship, and of its outcome was particularly noteworthy.

There were certain differences among patient attitudes and experiences resulting from the form of therapy which they received. The questions of whether the difference between psychoanalysis and psychotherapy is one of degree, as Alexander (1956) asserts, or one of kind, as a good many orthodox psychoanalysts assert, could not be answered by our study, although it appeared that the patients' experiences subtly shaded into one another. To employ Tarachow's (1963) distinction, it was clear that patients in goal-limited or brief psychotherapy viewed their therapists as real persons far more than did patients in more intensive psychotherapy (including analysis), where an "as-if" experience predominated. This finding is not surprising and merely confirms a long-held belief.

Patients' comments about their therapists varied to some extent depending upon the form of their therapy. The most enthusiastic (and perhaps least critical) reports came from patients in the less intensive forms of psychotherapy, whereas patients who received more intensive therapy tended to be somewhat more critical, cautious, and perhaps more realistic in their judgments. This response may be a function of the degree to which the therapeutic relationship itself became a topic for discussion in therapy. Highly enthusiastic endorsements of the therapist seemed to come primarily from patients who had experienced the therapist as a "real" person and whose therapeutic relationship had never become the focus of interpretation and scrutiny; more tempered evaluations were contributed by patients whose excessive expectations from the professional helper had been thwarted and who had suffered genuine disappointment as a result. It could not be determined whether the latter group achieved more lasting therapeutic gains and experienced more profound changes than the former. In general, however, a patient's favorable evaluation of his therapist was associated with a subjective experience of positive therapeutic gains, whereas negative attitudes toward the therapist were found to be associated with an unsatisfactory subjective experience of therapy. These negative attitudes apparently persisted well beyond the termination of therapy. Differences in the therapist's closeness to or aloofness from the patient, which stemmed from the technique that he employed, were overshadowed by this attitudinal variable, which appeared to be of crucial importance.

In addition to the differences attributable to the form of psychotherapy, we discerned the existence of an important selection factor. Apparently, patients were selected for intensive psychotherapy mainly on the basis of age (young patients were preferred), sex (male patients were preferred), and education (more highly educated patients were preferred), although other factors appeared to be involved as well: motivation to enter a prolonged therapeutic relationship, degree of disturbance, level of anxiety and discomfort, defensiveness, and other clinical considerations. Further elucidation of criteria for selecting patients for particular forms of psychotherapy, only suggested here, would be of the greatest value in adapting the method to the particular patient and his problem. It would also place the psychotherapeutic enterprise on a more secure scientific footing, as well as conserving time, energy, money, and professional manpower.

The patient's motivation for therapy has been mentioned as a factor in his selection for intensive therapy. A related problem concerns the motivational characteristics of patients who derived the greatest benefit from psychotherapy. Our data suggested that such patients had a positive therapeutic relationship and that those who were not too disturbed at the beginning of therapy were eager to work actively and seriously on their problems.

Correspondingly, the therapists' evaluations showed that they derived greatest enjoyment from treating patients with whom they had established a productive working relationship and that they preferred to work with patients whom they considered suitable for intensive psychotherapy, that is, those who had the greatest personality assets. This should not be interpreted to mean that they preferred patients who were not seriously disturbed; however, they tended to select those who, in their judgment, had the greatest potential for growth and change.

Irrespective of variations in the form of therapy and other considerations, the emergence of a "warmth" factor was particularly noteworthy. It permeated all ratings and assessments—those of patients as well as therapists. We concluded that a sense of mutual trust was unquestionably a *sine qua non* for successful psychotherapy; in its absence, little of positive value was accomplished. There was additional evidence that overshadowing this attitudinal-emotional factor was the patient's conviction that he had the therapist's respect. This faith in the integrity of the therapist as a person may be called the capstone of a successful therapeutic relationship under which all other characteristics are subsumed. When it existed, both patient and therapist were articulate about its presence.

We may speculate that technical skill on the part of the therapist may go a long way toward capitalizing on such a relationship once it exists, but we have little precise knowledge of how it comes into being, is deepened, or is used to maximum therapeutic advantage. Our work, as well as the research of others (e.g., Rogers et al. 1967; Truax and Carkhuff 1967), leaves little doubt that the kind of relationship described represents the basic ingredient of effective therapy, irrespective of the therapist's theoretical predilections and other factors. To assert the fundamental importance of the therapeutic relationship, however, is not to contend that it is the only factor affecting therapeutic change. It seems clear that some technical procedures are more effective than others, but the present investigation was not designed to shed light on that issue. It is likely that the most capable therapist is adept at creating and implementing working conditions which augur well for therapeutic progress and at selecting patients who have the potential for developing a productive working relationship. The relationship is basic, yet definition of what is learned within it—and, more important, *how* it is learned—is perhaps an equally large problem challenging the ingenuity of the researcher.

3.

THE PATIENT SPEAKS:
CASE HISTORIES

The group trends discussed in the preceding chapter and those of the second study, reported in later chapters, tell one side of the story. However, they cannot bring to life the stories of individual patients, with whom, in the final analysis, we are concerned. In this chapter, therefore, we present a selection of fairly typical case histories, drawn from both studies. Most of these accounts are from patients who expressed themselves favorably concerning their psychotherapy experience, but there are also some from persons who viewed their therapy experience as a failure. Not all respondents were as articulate as the ones whose questionnaire responses are discussed here, but the ones we chose are by no means unique.

Where comments from the therapist were available, they have been included. However, no attempt has been made to edit them or to reconstruct complete accounts using data from clinic files, which are commonly based on the objective and detached model of a medical history. While they often reveal a high level of sensitivity, sophistication, and perceptiveness, these patients speak as laymen, not professionals. Their reports may be distorted by self-deceptions, biases, and wishful thinking; they may be inaccurate when judged against objective criteria; they may reflect unresolved entanglements with the therapist or with other significant people in the person's life. Yet they are better than statistics and percentages at revealing not only pain, disappointment, suffering, and despair but also gratitude for having received help, acknowledgment of change for the better, and, in many cases, a sense of new courage and strength in facing the problems of life.

Mrs. Catherine Parks*

This patient, a young married woman aged 33 at the time of the study, had been seen in psychotherapy for a period of approximately three and a half years, two or three times a week. At the time of the questionnaire she was a housewife and portrait painter. She had two children. Family income was given as more than $12,500 a year. Her education included three years of college. Her therapy had terminated about two years before the survey was made. She described the complaints that led her to enter therapy as follows:

The term "worry yourself sick" applied to me. The weight of my many family illnesses and problems that were in areas where I was most vulnerable had led me to such repression of my worries that I was succumbing to a series of psychosomatic illnesses. I was in the hospital with Reynaud's syndrome when I decided things had gone far enough and entered therapy.

I should explain that I had so internalized my problems that no one thought I needed treatment except me. Only at the very last did even my husband recognize that my problems were overwhelming me.

* No patient's real name has been given.

She saw herself as rather anxious and said that she had experienced intense internal "pressure" to enter therapy. She was "extremely satisfied" with the results. When asked for the reasons for her satisfaction, she stated:

Heavens above! I could write a book! My whole life has changed and I now live comfortably with myself and my family. Not only this, I have had a baby—now eight months old—and this has brought us all a joy beyond words.

I am now at peace with myself. I no longer feel such a failure inside that I have to try to be 100% pluperfect on the outside and be all things to all men—so I can relax. I have discovered I'm more capable than I thought myself, for instance I have learned to paint and in fact paid for my treatment with money I made myself. I might add that I'm no longer quite so popular since I can now say "no" to my friends, but this doesn't bother me. I can pretty much take each day as it comes now and even derive much satisfaction from little things. Remaining problems include "factors that have nothing to do with me."

She considered the relationship with her mother as "still painful at times," but added: "I also realize that it is something to be lived with as best as I can." She felt that she was getting along very well and that her symptoms had completely disappeared. It was her impression that a fair amount of change had been apparent to her husband but none at all to other persons.

She thought that her therapist was interested in helping her but made it clear that the amount of improvement she made was the result of her own efforts. Her therapist was perceived as always polite, rather cool and impersonal, and very businesslike. Above all, she felt that he would help her to help herself. She admitted that often she felt like "just another patient," but added, "It was only after I could accept the fact that I *was* 'just another patient' instead of someone who had to be super special that I was on my way to being well."

A further comment was illuminating: "The therapist's attitude *was* rather stiff and formal—however, I took this to be his ordinary demeanor after a while, so I thought it perfectly natural. Some time after I completed therapy I met this doctor and his family socially and much to my surprise his personality was very unlike his professional personality. I have since decided that he varies his professional stance to best suit the personality of each patient."

Although she "mildly disagreed" with the statement that "nothing the therapist said or did ever decreased my self-respect," she added:

I consider this one of the turning points of my treatment. Through an inadvertent slip one day, the therapist did say something that absolutely crushed me for a day or so. This happened as I was leaving and in the intervening two days between this visit and the next I grew up at least ten years. I learned that, though hurt, I still lived, that someone for whom I had great regard could make a mistake too and that I could get angry without the world coming to an end or lightning striking me dead! In my next visit, the therapist explained it was a slip and apologized (incidentally, the only time he ever made a reference to himself) and I further realized I could forgive someone for hurting me.

Elaborating on being considered a "worthwhile person," she said: "Like any patient I was concerned with his feelings toward me, but as time went on I was less interested in his liking me than I was in liking myself. I came to realize that it doesn't really matter how 'worthwhile' you are in the conventional sense to a psychiatrist—if you are sincere and serious about your treatment he will do everything he can to help you even if you are the biggest louse there is in the community."

She attributed the success of her therapy to, among other things, the fact that she had taken the initiative and chosen her own therapist. She also recognized that her need for independence and her perfectionism, although they were closely bound up with her neurotic problems, at the same time provided the motivation for seeking professional help and the persistence in working on her difficulties over an extended period of time. Finally, she cited as a positive factor in her case the absence of a belief in God, which belief she thought accounted for the inability of many people to go beyond a supportive type of psychotherapy: "If one believes there is a God looking after one, it seems to leave a vacuum in the person when it comes to taking the basic responsibility for one's character and actions." In conclusion, she viewed the fact that she was able to take this responsibility and to turn to a professional person for help as "a *real* miracle and certainly a lesson to me *never* to underestimate the human spirit."

The therapist essentially agreed with Mrs. Parks's favorable evaluation of her treatment experience and termed the changes and the over-all success "fairly great." His comment, after reading her voluminous notes, was: "Thank goodness we have a few results like this to keep morale up and give the feeling it's really worth doing. This patient is really a very remarkable person." The account suggests that the results were at least partially due to her impressive personality assets and resources, which propelled her in the direction of a cure.

ARTHUR COLE

At the beginning of therapy this patient, a mathematician, was 32 years old and unmarried. He had earned the Ph.D. degree and at the time of the study was teaching at a university. He had been seen for 200 hours in psychotherapy over a period of almost two years. Interviews averaged three per week, and the therapist's fee was fifteen dollars per hour. He had left psychotherapy two years before answering the questionnaire because of external factors (the therapist was taking a sabbatical leave). He was moderately satisfied with the results of the treatment and credited himself with having obtained a certain amount of insight into some of his problems, but he thought that they were not worked out, which he attributed to the limited amount of time that was available. He stated that he had a need for further therapy but said the need was not "urgent," which fact, coupled with the expense, kept him from seeking it.

His presenting problem centered around a work inhibition, although he was aware of other major difficulties, such as family relationships and sexual problems, for which he hoped to obtain help. At the beginning of treatment, however, he carefully refrained from presenting these other difficulties to the therapist on the grounds that they would not be considered (presumably by the therapist) sufficiently important to warrant therapy. The therapist described Cole as rather schizoid, withdrawn, and aloof.

Cole considered his symptoms "somewhat involved" and noted appreciable change after about 4 months of treatment (about 50 hours). It appears that he developed a rather dependent relationship with his therapist, which he described in these terms: "My attitude toward him was somewhat similar (though not quite so strong) as that of a drowning person towards a log. Because of this, I purposely held back certain problems at the beginning of therapy and it took me quite a few months to persuade myself that the therapist was not on the verge—or would at least like to—kick me out of the therapy situation." At termination, he acknowledged that "I felt a little angry at being deserted but at the same time I had the full realization of how irrational the feeling was—I was a little embarrassed by it." He described his current attitude toward the therapist as "friendly."

Unlike most patients, he did not consider therapy an

intensely emotional experience, although he regarded it as often rather painful. He experienced relatively little feeling in the course of his therapy and did not recall ever being intensely angry at the therapist. He had a great deal of trust in the therapist's integrity and considered his attitude natural and unstudied as well as warm. He did not think that the therapist used technical language or that he engaged in small talk. He felt fully accepted and respected by him. His self-respect was never decreased during therapy.

Although he was convinced of the therapist's genuine interest in helping him, he had some question about the consistency of the therapist's attentiveness ("he was frequently hopelessly bored"). (A similar observation was made by John Starr, who was treated by the same psychiatrist. It is possible that this therapist employed an attitude of studied boredom as a therapeutic technique.) On the whole, he felt that the therapist was quite "active" and at times not averse to giving direct reassurance; still, he gave no advice to the patient on how to conduct his life.

There was the suggestion that in some respects this therapist emphasized intellectual understanding over the emotional aspects of the therapeutic experience. One comment by Cole may have some bearing on this: "I feel that a valid and important distinction can be made between intellectual insight into a problem and an emotional working through of it." He stated that he had gained intellectual insight into certain rather intensely hostile feelings towards persons "having a safely peripheral role in my life." In addition, he noted a growing sense of being an integrated person ("an organic whole changing gradually through time rather than a series of disjointed snapshots having no integral relation to each other"). Other gains included a reduction of his feelings of guilt about not being properly affectionate toward members of his immediate family, an awareness that he was lonely, a realization that he could play an active part in changing certain situations if he so desired, and a firmer sense of his masculine identity. His basic problems appeared to be unchanged, and he believed that no change had become apparent to other persons in his life. Still, he saw himself as getting along "fairly well" and felt "somewhat more able" to cope with his current problems.

Although he found it difficult to answer the question of his degree of identification with the therapist's attitudes, values, or opinions, he recognized—"sometimes to my surprise"—that he still finds himself using occasionally a certain phrase or sentence of the therapist. It is apparent that he approached therapy with a rather detached intellectual attitude. His therapist commented in his evaluation about Cole's remoteness. He rated his gains as moderate, noting that "he warmed up a good deal." Although limited in scope, the therapeutic results in this instance appear to be commensurate with the character structure of this patient.

Mrs. Suzanne Wilms

This rather seriously disturbed girl had been seen in psychoanalysis for a considerable period of time (five years) by one of the most experienced analysts participating in our research. She had been hospitalized for an acute schizophrenic episode prior to therapy. She was 18 years old when she entered therapy in 1954. Her rather wealthy parents initially paid for her treatment. While in therapy she completed her college education and married. At the time of the study she had one child, and her family income was rather modest.

Her questionnaire indicated that she had benefited from therapy to some extent, although she regarded herself in considerable need of further treatment. Fairly satisfied with the results, she now felt capable of viewing her situation in a more mature manner. However, a great number of symptoms still persisted, and she did not seem to be able to cope adequately with them.

Although she believed that her therapist was genuinely interested in helping her, she often felt she was "just another patient." She considered him stiff and formal and somewhat cold and distant, and she was never sure whether he considered her a worthwhile person. She had reservations about her trust in him, felt criticized at times, and recalled that he tended to talk about psychoanalytic theory during her sessions. In her words, "At the beginning I felt skeptical partially due to the procedure (saying 'whatever comes to your mind') and the relative coldness (and to my mind thus indifference) of the analyst; also some feelings of hostility and resentment despite a great desire for help." At the end of therapy she was "still somewhat mistrustful but I came to accept that this was due to a basic distrust of all persons; a far more friendly attitude prevailed." Now "few feelings of hostility remain and there is a general feeling of friendliness although I tend to blame the analyst for not 'helping me more.'" As for the specific ways in which the therapist effected change, she stated: "I do feel that his delving into my childhood experiences helped alleviate a number of unresolved guilt feelings; on the whole, however, I am not certain what aspect of his activities resulted in change." She believed that she identified with some of his attitudes and values: "His more liberal attitudes toward sex and religion were largely adopted by me; his attitude toward my family and his opinion that my life was my own and should be led as I saw fit were also taken over by me."

The problems which led Mrs. Wilms to enter psychotherapy were described as severe depression, inability to get along with friends, extreme irritability, feelings of hopelessness and despair, unexplainable feelings of fear, and very poor social adjustment. She viewed the disorder as chronic, thought she was getting along very poorly, and felt rather anxious and under extremely great "internal pressure." Through her therapeutic experience, she said, "My symptoms became meaningful; I had a great deal of understanding about my feelings and the reasons for them. However, I have since discovered the understanding was almost completely on an intellectual plane. Very little change (i.e., emotional) actually took place."

Although her gains from therapy appeared slight to her, she admitted having achieved a more realistic attitude toward her problems, and her symptoms, while still present, did not loom as large as they had and caused her less distress. The therapist in this instance took a more positive view of the outcome. He considered that the therapy had had "fairly great" over-all success and expressed a similar judgment concerning the degree of basic characterologic change. He felt he had a "fairly good" working relationship with Mrs. Wilms and had a "moderate" emotional investment in the treatment. After having examined her questionnaire responses he commented:

This patient had a severe paranoid schizophrenic disorder and was in the hospital prior to the commencement of psychotherapy with me. She made a limited improvement with reduction of guilt feelings and enhanced ability for reality-testing. At this time, she may be more amenable to a more psychoanalytic psychotherapy than was previously possible.

I am impressed that the patient indicates I used "technical terms." She had courses in psychology at _____ College and used some herself sometimes, but even so I think that what the patient regards as "technical terms" and what I would maybe were very much apart. Words were needed very much by this patient to name her feelings. There was, too, a difficult problem of silence for some periods, especially at the beginning of psychotherapy.

Although the success in this instance was only moderate, in view of the severity of her disturbance the therapist's evaluation may be the more realistic one.

At the end of the questionnaire Mrs. Wilms mentioned that she had recently applied for further therapy to the mental hygiene clinic in her community and that she was currently seeing a psychologist in psychotherapy. Her closing remarks were: "I feel it is too early to try to evaluate the results of my visits."

Mrs. Carole Barker

At the time of the study this patient was a high-school graduate, 34 years old, married, with one child. The family income was given as between $10,000 and $12,500 per year. Therapy had begun four years earlier, during a psychiatric hospitalization, the reasons for which she did not give: "I have never written down my symptoms. I feel a great reluctance toward doing so now—so I won't." At that time she was getting along very poorly, was very disturbed and anxious, and felt a great deal of internal pressure. Following her hospitalization, during which period she was seen daily, she was treated by the same therapist for a year on a once-a-week basis in face-to-face interviews, for which she paid five dollars per hour.

Although she did not seek further therapy thereafter, she felt in need of it a number of times; however, the distance between her home and the therapist's office was too great. She and her therapist decided to try treatment closer to home, but this arrangement did not prove satisfactory. Therapy was terminated by mutual agreement, but she still felt considerable need of it when she responded to the questionnaire.

She was fairly well satisfied with the results of her therapy. As she put it, "I made progress but was not cured,"

and added: "My problems to me were the same at the beginning and end of therapy. My hospitalization relieved
me, for a short period, of my domestic responsibilities,
therefore making them at least tolerable." She felt she had
changed somewhat as a result of psychotherapy: "I am no
longer getting treatment of any description. This was my
choice. I have been ill for such a long time now that I
cannot remember my life as it was before. The only
change I can describe at all is to tolerate the illness without getting hysterical." She said that the problems that
brought her to a therapist persisted, but she believed she
was dealing with them fairly adequately. What change she
was willing to admit was apparent to her husband, she said,
as well as to both close friends and acquaintances.

She remembered her therapy experience as intensely
emotional and painful and was unable to report a good deal
about it. She regarded her therapist as rather passive, stiff
and formal, cold, and unaccepting. She often felt like "just
another patient," complained about the therapist's inattention, and never felt sure whether he considered her a worthwhile person. She was not convinced that he was genuinely
interested in helping her. Her attitude was summed up in
an acerbic statement: "I loathed him, personally; respected
his ability." The passage of four years had not weakened
the intensity of her negative attitude, as she indicated: "I
still loathe him!" Elsewhere she said, "Some days I needed
reassurance. I'm sure I needed more than that but this is
what I was aware of. My therapist was cordial, but never
gave me any encouragement. My therapist's theory was
Silence." She denied having taken over any of his attitudes,
values, or opinions. "He had no opinions," she commented
wryly.

One surmises from these responses that the therapist
attempted to construct a therapeutic relationship on the
standard psychoanalytic model, which the patient (for rea-

sons of her own) experienced as vacuous and unhelpful. Apparently, she was never able to accommodate herself to the therapist's technique and left treatment in a rather acute state of negative transference, which never subsided. It seems that, while not unintelligent, she was rather obtuse in a psychological sense in making the analogy between her disturbance and a medical illness from which she would never recover.

For Mrs. Barker psychotherapy was basically not a worthwhile experience, and one cannot help wondering whether some modification in technique might not have produced a more favorable result. Her therapist felt that treatment of this patient had had "very little" success. He described his working relationship with her as "fairly poor" and characterized his over-all experiences with her as predominantly unpleasant:

Unfortunately this lady could not be seen more than once weekly. Each hour was isolated from the others. As soon as her defenses were threatened she became violently hostile and threatening. She had a severe obsessive-compulsive neurosis which covered vast reservoirs of hostility.

I had an opportunity to see her for one follow-up visit years later. She was unchanged—still using her symptoms to control mother, husband, and daughter, yet able to get out enough to enjoy life. As before, I recommended moving nearer to a source of therapy—and as before, she rejected this as impossible."

William Best

When he began therapy, this patient, 32 years old and unmarried, had completed two years of graduate study toward the M.S. in industrial relations and was about to receive the degree. He came from a fairly well-to-do family and was enrolled in a management training program for retail department stores. About age 17 he had a period of psychiatric hospitalization.

He was seen in intensive psychotherapy or psychoanalysis for almost five years, a total of between 400 and 450 hours. For the first six months interviews were conducted face to face; thereafter, he reclined on the couch. The usual fee was fifteen dollars per hour. Eight months after termination of the treatment he returned for 7 additional sessions. At the time of the study he felt no need for further intensive therapy but thought he could still benefit from a session now and then. He expressed himself as extremely satisfied with the results of his therapy and felt he had been much benefited. Before he came to the university he had received supportive therapy by several therapists. The last one encouraged him to seek intensive therapy, which he did.

His symptoms included anxiety about relationships with women, about doing well academically, and about relationships with parents and friends; obsessive-compulsive symptoms; lack of "emotional tone"; and bodily aches, physical symptoms, and frequent common colds. He believed his difficulties to be of long standing (five to ten years), experienced extremely great internal pressure and a fair amount of anxiety at the time of entering therapy, and thought he was getting along fairly poorly. Marked change became apparent to him about midway through treatment, after two years. At its termination he felt that his symptoms had been greatly alleviated and expressed the belief that they would completely disappear once he started working and got married.

He distinguished four areas of change which he attributed to his therapeutic experience: (1) increased "emotional tone," (2) increased insight, (3) increased understanding of others, and (4) external changes. He elaborated on these as follows: "I am now able to have 'pure' strong feelings. By pure I mean comfortable feelings. Thus, when

I was sick and *thought* I was happy at times it felt more like a nervous exhilaration or manic state rather than the feelings I have now which are truly comfortable and joyous and relaxing feelings. Likewise, now when I get angry I have a pure, strong feeling of anger. Expression of this anger brings relief. Anger makes me aggressive and makes me look for a solution and catharsis. Formerly, anger made me nervous, frightened, submissive, and eventually very depressed."

He had become able to be his "own therapist" and to handle formerly frightening or inexplicable feelings of fantasies. Other people had previously appeared to be "mysterious"; they seemed to know more about him than he knew about himself. Now, from what he had learned about himself, he felt he had an appreciation of the problems, fantasies, and motivations of others. He had fewer colds, slept much better, and had more physical energy. He still lacked full confidence in his own abilities but knew that he could succeed once he "got into the swing of things." Upon entering college he thought that he would "flunk out" but instead was elected to Phi Beta Kappa and went on to do graduate work. He believed that the change he experienced was obvious to his close associates but was less apparent to his co-workers and acquaintances.

This patient experienced therapy as an intensely emotional experience (he commented that this question sounded like one aimed at Park Avenue millionaires). He believed that the therapist was genuinely interested in helping him; he never felt like "just another patient"; the therapist seemed understanding and warm; he had many positive and complimentary things to say about his empathy, unequivocal honesty, "shocklessness," and unflagging attention. He commented on the therapist's ability to summarize trends without ever getting too far ahead of his patient. He was

aware of having identified with many of the therapist's
positive attributes—his love for truth and his desire to
understand people and their motivations. He developed a
great liking for the therapist and felt "a life-long bond"
with him; he admired his consideration and sense of humor;
and he had "complete confidence in him and no feelings
of hesitation about verbalizing or expressing any feelings or
thoughts." (The patient's trust in this therapist was a striking contrast to the negative comments of another patient,
Mrs. Carole Barker.)

In retrospect, he saw his problems as follows: "Repres-
sions (beginning about age 2½) which were heavily rein-
forced until about age 19 when I was first hospitalized. I
had 'learned' to deny most all my feelings. All my energies
which should have been used in a healthy, realistic way
were being bound up repressing feelings of hostility, jealousy, lust, attractions, etc., which I was unable to accept
or verbalize. Repressed feelings caused lack of emotional
tone. Repressed hostility caused depressions. Therapy en-
abled expression, verbalization and acceptance of childhood
fears, emotions, phantasies." The therapist described Best
as extremely anxious at the beginning of therapy. He had
expected some beneficial change and noted fairly great
symptomatic improvement upon termination, yet he felt
there had been only minor alteration of the basic personality structure. He felt that he had a fairly large emotional
investment in Best and described the working relationship
as "fairly good." He rated the therapy as a "moderate"
success. Beginning as largely supportive, it became intensive-analytical. He recalled both strikingly pleasant and
strikingly unpleasant experiences, and his laconic comment was that "in 5 years of intensive therapy of a schizophrenic one has all sorts of pleasant and unpleasant experiences!"

John Starr

This 28-year-old man, married with no children, was seen on a fairly intensive basis (three times a week) for a relatively short period of time (about a year). Like many patients represented in the sample, he had a high level of education—he had attended graduate school, without obtaining a degree—and held a managerial position in a contracting firm. His annual income was given as between $10,000 and $12,000. In therapy, both the couch and the face-to-face position were used at one time or another. The therapist described the form of therapy as gravitating toward the intensive-analytical pole. The patient described his problems as follows:

The symptoms which had begun 3–4 years prior to therapy included a sort of claustrophobia, especially in crowded places —I noticed that the intensity of these symptoms depended on how interested I was in something else, e.g., very little trouble at an exciting ball game, a lot of trouble during a dull sermon. Therefore, I was sure something could be done about it with competent professional help. The worst problem was that although I knew pretty well what was wrong, all logical methods of fighting it made it worse. It was like fighting a ghost— I knew there were no ghosts yet one had me on the run. Also, there were occasional migraine headaches (5–6 a year).

He thus appeared to have been under somewhat less strain when he entered therapy than many others in our sample.

He described himself as being extremely satisfied with the results of his treatment. He felt no need for further therapeutic work, thought he had changed a fair amount, and reported no problems that he could not cope with in one way or another. Commenting on the nature of the changes, he noted that only those closest to him had been able to notice them. He described what he considered perhaps the greatest change of all: "I have learned to accept myself as I am, and I find that I rather enjoy being me; the most drastic change, in other words, has been to learn that I can live an enjoyable life without any drastic changes. I do not mean that I now make no effort to improve myself; on the contrary, I think I am more intent on this than before. The difference is in my outlook and attitude more than anything else. As a result of the above, I find that I have more self-confidence, and am willing and able to tackle things that I would not have attempted before, though I may not like it any better."

Starr, at least in retrospect, had a fair amount of confidence in his therapist from the beginning: "I was looking for help and he was 'it,' as far as I was concerned." This feeling in itself, he said, was a very important ingredient in his progress. At the time of termination, the therapist recommended some further treatment, but he disagreed: "The therapist had done a better job than perhaps he realized, for I believed that I was far enough along to where I could work things out myself. I felt that my confidence in him was justified and that he had helped me a great deal." His comments indicate that the process of therapy often continues for a considerable period of time: "I feel that I am still improving as I go along, by applying what I learned while under treatment."

Although this patient was seen in intensive psychotherapy, the therapist did not follow the psychoanalytic model rigorously. Starr admitted feeling intensely angry at the therapist at times, but nothing the therapist said or did ever decreased his self-respect. He felt fully accepted as a worthwhile person, perceived the therapist's attitude as warm, and considered his interest genuine. The focus in therapy rested on his relationships with people in his current life, and one surmises that the therapist put little stress on the interpretation of transference feelings. Still, his technique was essentially interpretive, as the patient reported it, and he fully left the initiative with the patient: "His attitude showed that he was genuinely interested in helping me, but at the same time made it clear that most of it was up to me—he was neither overly friendly nor overly aloof—he was bored when the occasion would likely have bored most people, and somewhat enthusiastic at times, also." In sum, the therapist emerged as a fairly "real" person in therapy with his patient.

The therapist shared this evaluation and considered Starr markedly improved. The foregoing account is clearly an example of analytically oriented psychotherapy which bore fruit. Whether there were "basic" personality changes is questionable, but the symptomatic improvement was impressive.

Mrs. Jean Coates

This patient, a college graduate, married with four children, was working as an executive secretary at the time of the survey. Family income was given as between $12,500 and $13,000 per year. She had approximately 200 hours of psychotherapy at a rate of one to two sessions per week. At the time of the survey she had been out of treatment for about two years. She described the complaints that led her to enter therapy as follows: "Anxiety, constant kidney infection, frequent headaches, feelings of inadequacy about myself and my abilities. I felt that I was different and 'why does everything happen to me?' I thought if someone would just take all of these problems away from me, everything would be fine." She saw herself as extremely anxious prior to treatment and experienced intense internal pressure to enter therapy.

She was highly satisfied with the results for the following reasons: "I am better able to relate to others in a more

wholesome way. I have a greater degree of self-confidence
and independence. I have learned to cope with my situation in a more mature manner. Many old fears and anxieties
are no longer problems." She felt better able to accept herself and others and to give and accept love. She was more
willing to try new things, felt more confident and independent, and pointed with pride to the fact that during
therapy she had found a job at which she had steadily
advanced. At the time of the survey she was secretary to
the business manager of a large and complex business. She
felt able to make independent decisions now without lean-
ing on her husband excessively, as she had done prior to
treatment.

In summary, she said: "I have just gone through the experience of building a house with a minimum amount of
tension, especially since many well-meaning friends offered all sorts of free advice. I was able to follow through
with what I wanted and forget their advice. What's more,
my husband and I did not have a single major fuss during
construction as we were both able to work through differences of opinion to our mutual satisfaction."

While she saw herself as greatly improved and as getting
along extremely well on the whole, she listed some unresolved problems: "I still have feelings of inadequacy in
dealing with a teen-age daughter. I still feel some anxiety
when my husband is out of town, but I can live with it. I
still find myself at times playing the martyr. I still do not
have a healthy relationship with my oldest sister, but I don't
think I ever will. I react to her too much even now."

She felt some need for further therapy, but had not
sought it because of a "feeling that each time I cope
with a situation by myself, the greater my emotional
strength will be." For this woman, therapy had been an
intensely emotional and often rather painful experience.

While she was quite angry with the therapist at times, she felt sure that he was genuinely interested in her as a person, and she had absolute trust in him: "I feel that he is one of my best friends and that if I ever needed him, I could call him and by talking through my feelings, even by telephone, he would help me see the situation more realistically."

By her account, the therapeutic dialogue was focused on her attitudes and feelings toward the therapist, on early childhood experiences, and on current interpersonal relationships. In contrast to the majority of the respondents, major emphasis in her treatment had been on non-verbal communication, including gestures, bodily movements, silences, and the like. The therapist gave little advice or reassurance. She described him as "sympathetic, kind, understanding, persistent, and at times frustratingly evasive."

The therapist largely substantiated Mrs. Coates' view of the therapeutic experience. He described her as an extremely dependent person. Anger which developed as a result of frustrated dependency needs was characteristically turned inward and experienced as depression or physical illness. The therapist felt that the hostile, clinging aspect of her personality had been largely worked through during the course of therapy and cited as evidence the fact that she had obtained jobs with increasing responsibility and had developed various outside interests, such as becoming a member of the governing board at a large local church. He felt that she still had too great a need for approval but that she had "achieved a considerable degree of insight and has been able to accept some facets of her personality as inevitable; yet, she has been able to shift in a few others to the extent that life seems much more worthwhile to her now." He concurred with her decision to terminate therapy. The over-all success of the treatment was seen as fairly great by both the therapist and the patient. In this case, the therapeutic experience seemed to have been a mutually satisfying one.

Mrs. Elizabeth Norton

This 42-year-old woman, married with one child, had completed high school and attended business school for one year. At the time of treatment she was working as a stenographer, and the annual family income was less than $5,000. She had about 35 hours of therapy, usually once a week. The fee was five dollars per hour. She was treated by a resident, a mature man in his fifties. It should be noted parenthetically, however, that this man had been in general practice for many years and had taken up psychiatry relatively late in his career. A number of his patients had highly complimentary things to say about him.

Mrs. Norton expressed herself as "highly satisfied" with her therapy and felt she had benefited a great deal: "I felt my past therapy has given me something to fall back on, and if I feel I really need more, I will return; but with no major crisis I think I can manage on my own."

Her reasons for entering therapy were as follows: "I felt like there was no hope left in this life for me. There was no particular symptom other than mental confusion and loss of hope. I had terrible dreams, always waking up and wondering where I was. I lost my powers to concentrate on my work. I viewed my problems as such that if I didn't get some relief or change my attitudes toward my husband that life would be unbearable. There was depression and a feeling that I was about to lose contact with the world." It is significant that she experienced extremely great internal pressure to do something about these problems; that is, she was highly motivated to seek help.

She described the most important changes she experienced in these words:

I am more able to accept myself as I am and realize other people accept me for what I am. I realize at my age it is better to settle for what I have in the way of work, home, and my way of life than it is to always be pushing for something.

I still have very little self-confidence but I go ahead and accept positions in church work knowing that I am mentally capable, and with the hope that I can overcome the strong feelings of inadequacy.

On one or two occasions I have had the feeling that my husband could undo all by some attitude he has toward my feelings. I get the feeling when he is displeased that the world is about to crash around me.

The major change in my attitude came when near the end of my therapy I decided my husband would never change his feelings so I would seek another job and leave him. I had the self-confidence to try this. I had no real trouble finding another job and felt that if I could make this break with my old situation, everything would be better in the long run. Well, when I gave the news of my plans to my husband he remarked, "I'll be here all by myself in this house!" Well, the thought of his being left at home alone must have helped him realize he had to treat me like a person. There was a change in his attitude in that we can communicate now. There is no desire on my part for any sex life with him now although at the beginning of therapy that was one of my chief complaints—his lack of desire. I have the desire now as before but not for him. He only delivers disappointments. If my therapist had not given me the self-confidence to try to make this move to actually leave my husband, I would have continued through life wanting to try to leave but accepting defeat before trying. I tried to leave by getting the job in another city but I just could not leave him—he offers some kind of security, if not love and a normal married life—then something else I can't describe. I guess it is the fact that he is another living and breathing person to be accepted for what he is. Also, I could not bear the thoughts of living in an apartment and changing my way of life. I did not realize what these other things meant to me until I had the opportunity to leave. Without therapy I could never have accepted my present way of life as I do now. I am "stuck" with it and I'm going to make the most of it.

About her therapist she said:

I had a very personal feeling for him. I realized this for what it was and tried to keep my perspective but I hated to "give him up" at the end of therapy although I know there was nothing else he could do for me. I wanted to write him and thank him for the help given me but the letters were always too personal, so I destroyed them.

I really mean I would not want to be without the help given me and the things he told me during therapy. Things he made me bring out to myself revealed much to me. When the going gets rough I fall back on my memory of this experience to help me over. Getting over my feelings for the therapist was like "the cure was worse than the disease," but no fault of his.

As might be expected, she felt that the therapist was genuinely interested in helping her and respected her as a person; she never felt like "just another patient."

The clinic chart revealed that she was an only child. When she was 6 years old, her mother was sent to a state mental hospital, where she was still being cared for at the time of the survey. The patient went to live with her paternal grandparents. When she was about 7, her father died. After this she was cared for by a paternal uncle and his wife, who became her step-parents. During her childhood she felt considerable resentment against her stepmother, who was strict, punitive, and controlling.

Her hostility toward her husband seemed to stem in part from a lack of communication and in part from sexual advances she alleged he had made toward her 17-year-old daughter by a previous marriage. Frequent crying spells, fear of criticism, uncontrollable anger, and chronic depression were the principal symptoms. In one of her questionnaire responses she said: "I still can't listen to Christmas and Easter music in church without crying, but all these I can manage at this time." At the time of the survey, she had been out of therapy two years. The therapist noted that at termination the symptom of depression had disappeared.

4.

THE SECOND STUDY:
INTRODUCTION

Our second study was a more ambitious attempt to illumi-
nate the psychotherapy experience as seen by former patients. The earlier survey was based on data obtained from a
relatively small number of private patients who had been
seen over extended periods of time by highly experienced
therapists, and it seemed important to broaden our study
to a larger sample of clinic patients who, we hoped, would
make the survey representative of all individuals seen in
outpatient psychotherapy in this country today. We were
also interested in exploring further the extent to which
the findings about private patients applied to patients
treated at a psychiatric outpatient clinic.

The character of the assessments made by the therapists
was markedly different in the two studies. In Study 1
evaluations were made *ex post facto*, when it was undertaken, although therapists were asked to differentiate their
clinical evaluations of the patient "before" and "after"
therapy. This being the case, the degree to which the
therapist's assessments were contaminated by the shared

experience of the therapy itself as well as a host of other factors was unascertainable. Furthermore, it was reasonable to assume that therapists would rate patients whom they recalled having improved as more disturbed at the beginning of therapy than at the time of termination.

This problem was overcome by dispensing with the therapist's ratings altogether. Instead, both preliminary and final assessments were based on data from the patients' clinic charts. These data were not subject to distortions because they were gathered when the patient first came to the clinic, as well as at the end of therapy. The initial evaluations represented a consensus of the professional staff participating in the diagnostic conference, while final evaluations at termination were made by the therapist alone. The two groups of data were largely independent, and their value was undoubtedly enhanced by the fact that they had been made for routine clinic use rather than for a research project. There was no pressure on the therapist to fulfill the implicit expectations of the research staff. Accordingly, the assessments employed in Study 2 were clearly more objective than those in Study 1. Finally, a larger number of therapists and patients were involved than in the first survey. On the debit side, the data provided by the clinic charts were often incomplete. They consisted of narrative accounts, not ratings made on well-defined scales; they were written by therapists who employed varying criteria; and, unfortunately, they were sometimes entered in a slipshod fashion.

Thus, we have two sources of data in Study 2, questionnaires completed by former patients and information abstracted from clinic charts. The questionnaire was that used in Study 1 (see Appendix A), and a data sheet was designed to facilitate the collection of information from the clinic chart (see Appendix C).

THE CLINIC SETTING

The patient sample was drawn from the files of the Adult Psychiatric Outpatient Clinic at North Carolina Memorial Hospital, the training facility of the University of North Carolina School of Medicine. The clinic, which is similar to many others throughout the country, provides diagnostic and treatment services on a low-cost basis to persons over 16 years of age. Younger patients are seen in the Child Clinic, located in the same building. The usual treatment may be characterized as brief individual psychotherapy on a once-a-week basis by a therapist in training. Tabulations of completed therapy for a recent twelve-month period showed that 696 patients had terminated, of whom only 91 had been seen for twenty interviews or more. Actually, only 257 persons in this group had been referred to this clinic for treatment; the balance consisted of persons who had been referred for diagnostic evaluations and similar reasons.

Although treatment at the clinic is usually brief, the intensive psychodynamic approach is the preferred model. Students are taught that neurotic symptoms and personality patterns are forms of learned behavior which do not readily yield to simple advice, drugs, or magic. It is recognized that the patient needs to develop trust and confidence in the therapist. In the context of this supportive relationship, the patient learns to observe and identify self-defeating aspects of his behavior. The goal is to help develop alternative modes of coping with stress.

This model obviously calls for therapy over extended periods of time, although practical considerations often militate against it. For example, of some 450 patients seen in one year, a substantial percentage terminated treatment within 12 months. Pfouts, Wallach, and Jenkins (1963) reported that the clinic serves as a diagnostic center for the majority of its patients and as a treatment center for only a few, and commented: "Too often policies and procedures are set up as if the clinic were almost exclusively a long-term intensive treatment center, when in reality it is for the majority of the patients a diagnostic and brief therapy center." For these reasons, patients selected for our sample cannot be regarded as a cross-section of all patients seen at the clinic.

SELECTION OF THE PATIENT SAMPLE

Patients were selected for inclusion in the sample if they had been seen for 25 interviews or more by a resident in psychiatry, an advanced graduate student in clinical psychology, or a staff member (a psychiatrist or a clinical psychologist), and had left therapy at least one year prior to the beginning of the study.

The requirement of 25 interviews was imposed because we wished to concentrate on individuals who had remained in therapy for a reasonable period and for whom therapy might be presumed to have been a significant experience. By eliminating early dropouts we also hoped to obtain a more homogeneous sample of stayers. A time lapse of one year after termination of therapy was imposed to obtain a clearer picture both of the nature of the therapeutic changes and of their durability.* The sample was restricted

---

* While the research evidence is sketchy, there is good reason to believe that the consolidation of therapeutic gains requires a considerable period of time—sometimes as much as four to five years (Schjelderup 1955). Most published studies of therapeutic outcomes ignore this observation and make evaluations immediately following the termination of therapy. This is often a period of upheaval and stress, marked by the temporary reactivation of old symptoms and disturbances, and is particularly trying when therapy has lasted for a long period of time and an intense transference relationship has been established. The resolution of the patient's attachment to

to patients of advanced students and staff to standardize
the experience level of the therapists: a large proportion
of this clinic's patients were routinely seen by medical
students.

DATA COLLECTION

At the beginning of August, 1964, 244 questionnaires
were mailed to former patients. The mailing yielded 92
completed questionnaires. A follow-up mailing about a
month later produced 39 more questionnaires, bringing
the total to 131. Table 1 summarizes these data. The rate
of return (excluding undeliverable letters) was 64 per
cent—quite high for surveys of this kind. The number of
therapists represented was 79; the range of patients per
therapist was from one to five, with a median of one.

Table 1. Summary Results of Questionnaire Returns

Result	N	%
Returned completed	131	53.7
Returned refused	17	7.0
No reply	57	23.3
Undeliverable	39	16.0
Total	244	100.0

PATIENT SAMPLE

The Question of Sample Bias

As pointed out earlier, the patient sample used in this
study cannot be considered representative of patients at
the Psychiatric Outpatient Clinic at North Carolina Memorial Hospital. As a group our subjects did not differ

the therapist revives problems of separation which may be exceedingly painful and may obscure permanent changes that will appear
in clearer form later on.

markedly from the group of long-term private patients in Study 1 except in financial resources. The similarity between the two groups extended to such variables as level of education, cultural background, motivation for therapy, psychological-mindedness (the ability to maintain distance from one's problems and to view them as disturbances in interpersonal relationships), nature and severity of disturbance, sense of social responsibility, and the like. Still, it was necessary to determine whether the individuals who completed the questionnaire differed in some characteristic way from those who failed to respond, refused to collaborate, or had moved without leaving a forwarding address. For example, it was possible that patients who had completed the questionnaire were more satisfied with their therapy experience and outcome than the others.

In the majority of instances we found that no systematic bias existed (see Appendix D). However, we found that the patients who failed to reply or refused to reply tended to be more impaired in their psychological functioning, had a poorer prognosis, were more likely to have had prior hospitalizations (irrespective of length), and were likely to have been referred by a psychiatrist or the Inpatient Service of North Carolina Memorial Hospital, rather than a family physician or a general medical hospital. Less disturbed patients were therefore somewhat over-represented in the completed questionnaires.

Rater Agreement on Judgments from Clinic Charts

Numerous items of information extracted from patients' clinic charts for purposes of this study were sufficiently objective to require a minimum of professional interpretation. In addition, however, members of the project staff, working independently, integrated various items of information contained in the charts. We found that the rater agreement was not uniformly high, but there was a reasonable consensus on the key variable, over-all success (see Appendix E).

Biographical and Socioeconomic Data

Table 2 presents a biographical and socioeconomic breakdown of the patient sample at the beginning of therapy and at the time of the survey. (Because of incomplete responses or similar reasons, 9 protocols were excluded, leaving a total sample of 122.) Females were somewhat over-represented: while the normal clinic load was almost evenly divided between men and women, women comprised 60 per cent of our sample (73 patients).

At the beginning of treatment the sample was equally divided between married and single persons. Despite the popular belief that psychotherapy often results in divorce, Table 2 indicates that this outcome was virtually non-existent. Since we were dealing with young adults, it is not surprising that the number of married persons increased from 56 to 69 over the years.

In the occupational category, we should note that 53 respondents were students when entering therapy and that only 7 were employed in service, agricultural, mechanical, or manual work. At the time of the questionnaire, the number of students had dropped to 15, but 29 persons were engaged in professional-technical occupations. Because of the number of patients who were still students when the survey was made, the relative frequency of professional-technical occupations is probably underestimated. The number of unemployed patients dropped from 12 to 3 at the end of the survey.

The gross annual income reported in the table is probably not an adequate index of the patients' economic level. The data concerning income were obtained for the purpose of setting a fee and determining eligibility for clinic treatment; thus it is likely that the reports are underestimates.

Table 2. Biographical and Socioeconomic Data

Variable	At Beginning of Therapy		At Time of Survey	
	N	%	N	%
Sex				
Male	49	40.1	49	40.1
Female	73	59.9	73	59.9
Marital status				
Single	56	45.9	42	34.4
Married	56	45.9	69	56.6
Divorced	7	5.7	8	6.5
Widowed	3	2.5	3	2.5
No. of children				
Unknown	—	—	3	2.5
0	73	59.9	56	45.9
1	13	10.6	19	15.5
2	20	16.4	21	17.2
3	14	11.5	18	14.8
4	2	1.6	4	3.3
5	—	—	1	0.8
Occupation[a]				
Student	53	43.4	15	12.2
Housewife	27	22.2	25	20.5
Professional	9	7.4	29	23.8
Manual	7	5.7	14	11.5
Clerical	11	9.0	24	19.7
Unemployed	12	9.8	3	2.5
Unknown	3	2.5	12	9.8
Gross family income				
Unknown	83	68.0	5	4.1
Under $5,000	23	18.9	50	41.0
$5,000–$7,500	11	9.0	34	27.9
$7,500–$10,000	3	2.5	17	13.9
$10,000–$12,500	0	—	12	9.8
$12,500–$15,000	0	—	3	2.5
Over $15,000	2	1.6	1	0.8
Age				
18–21	35	28.7	4	3.3
22–25	20	16.4	29	23.8
26–29	19	15.5	18	14.8
30–33	18	14.8	16	13.0
34–37	11	9.0	21	17.2
38–41	10	8.2	14	11.5
42–45	4	3.3	10	8.2
46–49	4	3.3	4	3.3
Over 50	1	0.8	6	4.9
Education				
Less than high-school grad.	14	11.5	14	11.5
High-school grad.	27	22.2	23	18.9
Some college	57	46.7	37	30.3
College grad.	11	9.0	30	24.5
Grad. study	13	10.6	18	14.8

[a] As defined by the *Dictionary of Occupational Titles*.

In view of the importance of this item for clinic purposes, it is surprising that it was recorded in the clinic charts of only 39 patients. The fact that 23 members of this group reported annual income of less than $5,000 probably reflects the large number of students in the sample. Only 5 respondents failed to report their gross annual income. The modal income of the 117 who reported it was less than $5,000, although 34 were earning between $5,000 and $7,500 and 33 were earning $7,500 or more.

The low modal income probably reflects the fact that many of these young adults had not yet reached the peak of their earning power. The modal age in the sample was 18–21 and the mean age 28.3. Only 5 persons were over 45 years of age when they began treatment. (88 per cent of all patients admitted and terminated at this clinic in a typical year were under 45).

The educational level of the sample was obviously high: two-thirds of the patients had at least some college experience. At the time of the survey the number of persons who had not graduated from high school remained the same, but there were 30 college graduates and 18 persons working on advanced degrees.

About one-half of the patients lived within a radius of twenty-five miles from the clinic, but an appreciable number traveled considerable distances to obtain therapy, probably at marked expense, inconvenience, and sacrifice of time.

Form and Length of Psychotherapy

Table 3 details the course of treatment for the experimental sample.

The majority of the patients were seen in therapy once a week, although a substantial percentage (34 per cent) were seen twice. It was rare for any patient to be seen less than once or more than twice a week. Most of the

Table 3. Course of Treatment

Variable	N	M
Therapeutic hours per week		
Less than 1	7	
1	66	
2	42	1.4
3	6	
Unknown	1	
Total therapeutic hours		
25–49	54	
50–74	26	
75–99	14	
100–124	10	70.4
125–149	5	
150–174	2	
175–199	2	
200 or more	4	
Unknown	5	
Number of therapists		
1	99	
2	18	—
3 or more	5	
Treatment after discharge		
Yes	28	
No	93	—
Unknown	1	
Previous psychiatric hospitalization		
Yes	48	
No	59	—
Unknown	15	
Drugs used during therapy		
Yes	25	
No	92	—
Unknown	5	

patients received between 26 and 49 hours of therapy, about 6 or 12 months of treatment at the average rate of one or two sessions a week. By definition, then, this therapy was neither intensive nor long-term. By far the majority of patients (99) were seen by only one therapist during their course of treatment. However, 18 patients had two therapists and 5 had three or more.

Approximately 23 per cent of the sample received further treatment after leaving the clinic. The questionnaires indicated that 16 were currently in treatment with private psychiatrists and that 3 had been in treatment which had terminated. In spite of the fact that only 20 per cent of all patients referred to the clinic had histories of hospitalization for mental disorders, 48 of the persons in our sample (39 per cent) had such histories. Table 3 indicates that some time after the termination of clinic therapy 7 patients had been hospitalized but they were not in treatment at the time of follow-up; 2 others had been hospitalized and were still under the care of a psychiatrist.

Statistical Treatment of the Data

The statistical treatment of the data, in which the therapist's appraisal of outcome and the patients' self-ratings are key variables, is described in Appendix F. It may be objected that when a patient and his therapist arrive at a consensus on the outcome of the therapy, the patient's subjective feeling of having been helped and the therapist's parallel appraisal of improvement do not prove that the therapeutic experience has in fact been a success. More objective data, such as the patient's performance on the job, his handling of interpersonal situations, and so on, if they had been available, would be more convincing; however, in their absence, the patient's feeling of relief and increased sense of competence and adequacy is a valid index of improvement in its own right.

In view of this greater incidence of prior psychiatric hospitalization in the experimental sample, it is not surprising that drugs were used in combination with psychotherapy more often than in the general clinic population. Drugs were prescribed at some time during the course of treatment for 20 per cent of the patients in the sample, as opposed to 10 per cent of the general clinic population. In terms of hospitalizations and administration of drugs, then, patients in the experimental sample seemed to be somewhat more disturbed than the average clinic patient. However, since the discharge summaries of hospitalized patients tended to contain more information than was available for general clinic admissions, these detailed descriptions and assessments may have played a part in bringing such patients to the therapists' attention and thus in their eventual acceptance for prolonged outpatient therapy.

The questionnaires indicated that most respondents had taken the survey seriously and had written fully and candidly about their psychotherapy. It appeared that many patients welcomed the opportunity to rethink the experience and to put into words feelings that they had not previously formulated to themselves or to others. We were impressed by the spontaneity of their comments and regarded them of a value equal to—if not greater than—their responses to the structured questions. Consequently, we made extensive use of this material and attempted to determine and systematize its common elements (see Appendix G).

5.

THE PATIENT'S VIEW

Presenting Symptoms

According to a popular misconception, people go to psychiatrists primarily for severe mental disorders whose symptoms are apparent to everyone. While severe distress is certainly a powerful motivating force, it may go virtually unnoticed even by persons close to the patient. However, many respondents in our survey entered treatment because of less dramatic problems which had eaten away at their peace of mind, pride, and zest for life, problems which are a part of everyone's life from time to time but which they experienced with unusual intensity or persistence, with a resultant profound sense of helplessness. It was primarily this generalized unhappiness and estrangement from life which motivated the patients in our survey to turn to a psychiatrist or a clinic for help.

In the questionnaires expressions like "dissatisfaction" and "lack of purpose or involvement" recurred and reflected this concern. One patient said: "I seemed to have lost interest in everything and everybody in my life. I was extremely tired and weak all of the time and I couldn't face my responsibilities. I had a very hopeless outlook on my problems at the beginning of therapy." Another said he experienced "just complete unhappiness with life. I didn't know what my problems were. All I knew was that I was very miserable for some reason."

In addition, and seemingly unrelated to these complaints, were more specific feelings of being unable to meet the ordinary demands of living. People reported hopelessness, discouragement, or a feeling that life was passing them by. Their vague feelings often were sufficiently painful in and of themselves to constitute a motive for seeking help. Sometimes they blamed feelings of inadequacy, tension, anxiety, nervousness, and generalized fears for their discomfort.

One man said: "I felt complete dissatisfaction with life as it was for me. I had no idea of what I wanted to do or in what direction I was going. This bothered me a great deal. Although I made several attempts at trying to find myself, I became impatient at my inability to do so. This resulted most of the time in a 'don't give a damn' attitude which resulted in excessive drinking, idleness, scrapes with death, the law and insanity." Another said: "I was extremely nervous and sensitive, to the point that I couldn't really concentrate, I had almost no grasp on anything, and it made things so miserable that I felt I *had* to have some help." One woman was "constantly nervous and upset and it became so intense that I had to have someone to confide in."

Virtually all patients listed multiple symptoms. Figure 1 shows a tabulation of the major complaints which led them to enter psychotherapy.* Prominently mentioned were loss of interest in day-to-day living and an inability to

* A discussion of how the content areas were derived and the rationale for the particular scheme used is presented in Appendix G. The aim was to devise a phenomenological grouping of initial complaints as the patient described them. A single complaint may be

MAJOR COMPLAINTS BRINGING PATIENTS TO THERAPY

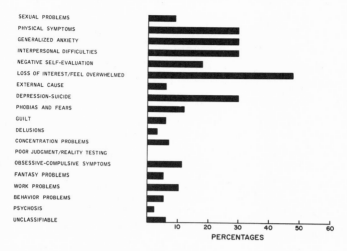

Figure 1

meet daily responsibilities. Also mentioned with high frequency were physical symptoms, generalized anxiety, interpersonal problems, and depressive feelings (both with and
without suicidal thoughts). Less frequent but still common
were complaints of sexual problems, specific phobias and
fears, obsessive-compulsive thoughts or behaviors, and work
difficulties.

The quest for treatment is not the result merely of a
philosophical or reflective process, along with the realization that things are not as they should be and that one is
not living up to his own aspirations. The people we questioned were impelled by a considerable amount of anxiety
and internal pressure to do something about themselves.
The uneasiness and tension became noticeable and grew
until it became a serious burden. In short, they were

listed in more than one category in order to capture as many
nuances of the written comment as possible.

persons suffering. After many tortuous attempts to regain their equilibrium on their own, they finally conceded defeat and recognized the need for professional help. This state was captured in part by one patient: "I seemed unable to concentrate and was somewhat without feelings. I knew something was wrong but I had no idea what. At first I felt it was worry over finances as things piled up. I was expecting a second child, which was solely my idea, and I thought this could have something to do with the way I felt. The hours were so long, even the minutes were long, I was afraid, very much afraid."

The sequence of experiencing anxiety, searching for solutions, and failing to find them may go on for quite a long time before a person seeks professional help. Over half of the patients in our study were aware of difficulties for more than a year before they took action, and many others delayed for more than two years.

For most people seeking psychiatric help is a humiliating process. It means giving up self-direction and placing oneself in a dependent position. For many persons psychotherapy remains a strange and unknown treatment. It forces people into the very situation many of them have been trying to avoid—a close interpersonal relationship. For these reasons and others, it takes a long time for a prospective patient to enter a clinic or therapist's office. The crucial importance of a person's first contact with the treatment agency is also clear.

During a typical year only 11 per cent of new patients came to the Psychiatric Outpatient Clinic on their own. Most people, as was pointed out in the Report of the Joint Commission on Mental Illness and Health, were referred by sources outside the field of mental health. In times of trouble they are likely to consult their family physician, who may refer them to a private practitioner or a clinic. While ignorance of therapeutic facilities may play its part, people do tend to try to find a physical or organic basis for their emotional problems.

Degree and Chronicity of Disturbance

One's memory for pain is short-lived and not too reliable. The pain accompanying neurotic suffering is often dull rather than acute, and it may persist for a long time before the afflicted person enlists professional help. Psychic pain can be as severe as physical pain, and it may be aggravated by the fact that the sufferer does not know its location or cause. In general, pain serves an adaptive function by alerting one to the fact that something is amiss and that help is needed. Of the kinds of pain which focus a person's attention upon himself, anxiety is probably the most common. Patients who enter psychotherapy without experiencing a significant amount of anxiety are poor prospects, as are patients who are overwhelmed by it. Luborsky (1962) has shown that there is an "optimum" level of anxiety which seems to provide the best motivation for entering psychotherapy, actively participating in the treatment process, and experiencing a satisfactory outcome.

Pain, to be sure, is a subjective experience and it is difficult to compare one person's pain with that of another. The same is true of people's tolerance for pain, which is also highly subjective. One person, for a host of reasons, some of which are part and parcel of his neurotic problems, may search eagerly for a relationship that promises relief of his suffering; another individual may suffer in silence for years. Suffering itself, of course, may provide neurotic gratifications to which a person may cling with tenacity. Nevertheless, it is instructive to examine how former patients viewed their predicament in retrospect; in addition, such data may be helpful in assessing therapeutic outcomes.

Patients were asked to rate the degree of disturbance, the

amount of anxiety, and the internal pressure they experienced at the beginning of treatment. They were also asked for estimates of how well they were getting along at present and how long they had felt in need of professional help before coming to the clinic. The answers reveal that 69 per cent of the patients believed themselves to have been more than moderately disturbed at the beginning of treatment. The vast majority had experienced intense anxiety and considerable internal pressure to do something about their problems. Only 8 per cent felt that they were getting along at least "fairly well" when they entered treatment, an indication of the extreme discomfort and life disruption attendant upon the decision to seek help. Some 39 per cent dated the onset of their difficulties less than a year prior to the beginning of psychotherapy, but 27 per cent regarded them as of long standing.

Assessments of Therapeutic Outcome

Because of its central importance, the questionnaire dealt with several facets of the problem. While the patients may have felt that the researchers were asking for testimonials, they were certainly under no compulsion to give them, and their anonymity was a further invitation to candor.

Questions pertaining to the amount of benefit the therapy afforded them (Item 18), their opinion of the results (Item 19), and the degree of change they observed (Items 73 and 79) yielded very comparable responses: approximately three out of every four patients considered their psychotherapy a worthwhile experience. The complaints or symptoms that brought them to the clinic had not completely disappeared, but there was little question in their minds that there had been marked improvement.

We see no reason to take issue with these reports, which provide impressive evidence in favor of the kind of therapy practiced at this clinic. We shall reserve for later discussion the question of whether improvement would have occurred even without psychotherapy. At this point, we merely wish to note that a substantial percentage of patients reported marked improvement, were satisfied with the professional service they received, and attributed the changes they reported to the psychotherapeutic experience. The questions and responses to these four questionnaire items are given below.

18. *How much have you benefited from your therapy?*

	N	%
A great deal	72	59
A fair amount	22	18
To some extent	18	15
Very little	5	4
Not at all	5	4

19. *Everything considered, how satisfied are you with the results of your psychotherapy experience?*

	N	%
Extremely dissatisfied	4	2
Moderately dissatisfied	6	5
Fairly dissatisfied	3	2
Fairly satisfied	12	10
Moderately satisfied	30	25
Highly satisfied	36	30
Extremely satisfied	28	24
[No response]	[3]	[2]

79. *To what extent have your complaints or symptoms that brought you to therapy changed as a result of treatment?*

	N	%
Completely disappeared	7	6
Very greatly improved	42	35
Considerably improved	29	24
Somewhat improved	25	20
Not at all improved	11	9
Got worse	2	2
[No response]	[5]	[4]

73. *How much do you feel you have changed as a result of therapy?*

	N	%
A great deal	54	44
A fair amount	37	30
Somewhat	16	13
Very little	6	5
Not at all	8	7
[No response]	[1]	[1]

Marked improvement within 12 months after entering therapy was reported by 67 per cent of the respondents. This finding must be qualified by the fact that most patients in this sample were in treatment for only 6 to 12 months. There is also reason to believe that a fair amount of guess-work influenced the responses, since it is probable that few patients had precise recollections on this point. It is hardly surprising that therapeutic changes were reported to occur gradually rather than dramatically.

80. *How soon after entering therapy did you feel any marked change?* (Responses were categorized subsequently.)

	N	%
1– 3 months	33	27
4– 6 months	22	18
7–12 months	27	22
13–18 months	3	2
19–24 months	5	4
25+ months	2	2
No improvement	13	11
[No response]	[17]	[14]

It is noteworthy that these clinic patients were no less satisfied with their therapy experience than the private patients in Study 1, who had been seen by more highly experienced therapists over a longer time period (Strupp, Wallach, and Wogan 1964). Of course, we do not know whether their expectations were different or whether they applied the same criteria. Although the clinic patients tended to see themselves as somewhat more disturbed, and their assessments of therapeutic outcomes were just a shade less favorable, the similarities between the two samples are more impressive than the differences. A majority in both groups was willing to recommend psychotherapy to others (see Appendix A, Item 88).

PATIENTS' EVALUATIONS OF THERAPEUTIC CHANGE

Having considered over-all assessments of improvement, we are now ready to examine more closely the kinds of changes reported by our respondents. Open-ended responses were classified by the same system used for coding initial symptoms, thus permitting direct comparisons. Figure 2 shows the parallel percentage distributions.* We shall comment on the more prominent categories.

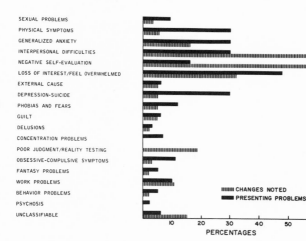

COMPARISON OF MOST IMPORTANT CHANGES
EXPERIENCED AND PRESENTING PROBLEMS

Figure 2

* Presenting complaints are identical in Figures 1 and 2; they are repeated for ease of comparison.

Better Interpersonal Relations

Improvements in interpersonal functioning were noted with the greatest frequency. As problems in this area were by no means the most common complaints, the conclusion is justified that, as might be expected, problems and difficulties in interpersonal relationships became a major focus of inquiry during the course of therapy.

The therapists' theoretical orientation and their approach to psychotherapy is reflected here. Instead of centering on presenting symptoms, the therapist confronted the patient with his conflicts and neurotic patterns in his relations with significant persons in his life. The result, at least in part, was that the patients came to view their difficulties as problems in living rather than manifestations of a mysterious force. Whether this cognitive understanding was always, or even regularly, accompanied by emotional "insight" is of course uncertain; however, it is likely that cognitive appreciation by itself changes little unless it is accompanied by an emotional experience within the framework of the therapeutic relationship. Some typical descriptions of such changes are given below.

1. I can love my daughter without reservation. 2. I have no animosity toward my mother as I once had. 3. I'm not afraid to experience unpleasant emotions and can do so without a feeling of guilt. 4. I'm not afraid to stand up for myself and to voice my opinions.

I have more *true* patience and understanding of myself and others—I don't lose my temper as often—and I feel contented and very happy and glad to be alive. I feel very much aware of life and the feelings of others. My children are happy go lucky and seem to me to be normal as children go. I'm also aware of my husband and his needs and our life together seems richer.

I look on sex quite different now—can be around men without quite as much fear as before. These two changes have let

me trust someone enough that I finally let my feelings come
to the surface, to love someone enough to marry.

Have been able to lead a full, active and constructive life
with many personal relationships that have been very satisfying, and quite a few that might have been upsetting but which
I managed to handle fairly well, I think, at least so far as I
personally was concerned. Can accept philosophically and with
some degree of understanding others' anger toward me and
can express my anger more constructively.

I like being around other people which I did not before. I
can detach myself from family problems (mother and sister)
more easily and am not so quick to condemn them or offer
advice. Many times I put myself in the position of a "therapist" and listen—and try to understand other people's problems as they relate to them rather than to myself.

The change from striving to do things that boys do to becoming interested in things girls do. The deep subconscious
change or really realization that I am a girl, and I think for the
first time in my adult life, I was glad it was so. I also dropped
my innermost guard against letting anyone really get close to
me. I dared to look out and up and hope. I changed basically
from a pessimist to an optimist. I grew enough to be willing
to want to give of myself—to realize I needed others. To be
able much of the time to consider others before myself. To
be able to wish them well, warmly and sincerely even when it
was not what I wanted. Another big change was one of really
listening or involve myself, now I find I see people in a different light. I have become open-minded with opinions but not
judgments. Realizing we all have good and bad qualities and
to others "clayfeet" at times.

Increase in Self-Esteem

Mentioned with almost equal frequency were changes sig-
nifying an increase in self-confidence, security, self-respect,
and personal worth. These improvements may perhaps be
viewed as by-products of personality or behavior changes
that occurred during psychotherapy and resulted in a re-
vised self-evaluation. The latter may be the outcome of

the following modifications (and probably others): (1) The patient actually performs more adequately in interpersonal relationships (both as he sees his performance and as it is reflected to him by others) and thus gains greater self-respect. Similarly, he may feel less hostile or hateful as a result of the therapy experience, hence less disposed toward guilt and self-condemnation for harboring these feelings. (2) The patient's performance or feelings may remain unchanged, yet he may feel less critical either of his behavior or feelings.

In either event, the outcome is a more harmonious alignment between inner pressures and reality demands. Identification with a more tolerant, accepting, and realistic standard as communicated by the therapist probably plays an important part in this process. Other factors may also be instrumental in enhancing a patient's self-esteem, but changes in a person's self-concept, while difficult to qualify, must be counted among the most important achievements of psychotherapy. Some typical quotations exemplify our patients' responses:

I think the greatest change has been getting my confidence back and being able to lead a normal life. Since I stopped my therapy I have experienced 3 deaths in my family, one of which was my mother's three weeks ago, and three years ago I feel I would not have been able to go on. I believe I can reason things out better now and even if I make a mistake I try to realize that this is life and no one can be right all of the time.

It is so hard for me to explain my feelings but I'm sure I'm a different person in attitude. I feel so much more relaxed—more confident, sure of myself, more attractive, and above all, my husband and my daughter enjoy me more. I now drive a car (learned while coming to Memorial) and can do things I never dreamed I could do. I strongly recommend help of this kind for anyone slightly disturbed.

My self-evaluation is much higher, but I do suffer from some guilt complex still. My problem itself has not left me, or even been relieved, but I have learned to face reality and to accept myself more as I am. I'm sure therapy was the most important factor of this change.

I am much more at ease among groups of people than I was before my therapy. I now feel capable of accomplishing certain goals which I formerly regarded as desirable, but unattainable, dreams. I rarely need tranquilizers (or beer) to cope with tension.

I feel confident, have no guilt feeling and feel very capable and have a deeper richer meaning to life as a result of psychotherapy.

I have accepted "me." I know now everyone experiences anxiety and uses an individual mechanism to accommodate this. I understand my own particular pattern and can adjust accordingly.

I still have spells of incapacitating anxiety when confronted with large tasks, but have managed to face up to two major tasks successfully—Ph.D. orals and written exams. Perhaps I have found that I needn't be as good as I once thought I had to be in order to get by or to be accepted. Perhaps I have more faith and courage now than I had before. Also I am more willing to understand and to accept others (though still not very willing at times).

I do not feel so gloomy, worried, and undecided as I did before. I am more self-confident, and I have gained much strength in standing for what I think best.

1. Ability to accept myself. 2. Ability to accept others and try to understand them. 3. Ability to give and accept love. 4. Willingness to try new things. 5. Development of confidence and independence (found a job, have been steadily advanced in job since—and I make decisions during a day without consulting husband).

Greater Interest in Living, Energy, and Satisfaction

This heading essentially refers to diminution of anxiety and neurotic suffering in general. If beneficial changes were noted by a respondent, they were almost certain to be included in this category. Admittedly, this tells us little more than that the patient felt better:

I've become more aggressive in life, learned to live with normal pressures and problems without getting petrified, and we've finally got a darling, healthy baby girl.

The most important change, I think, has been letting go of my own fantasies and facing my situation and experiences for what they are. I had always been a suspicious person, looking for someone to hurt my feelings, and then dwelling on it. Then, too, I'm able to find satisfaction and happiness in small ways that I had always overlooked before, probably because I was too busy worrying about myself. In many ways I'm an idealistic person and perhaps the most important change in me has been learning the difference between things as they are and things as I think they should be.

I have a moderate amount of satisfaction now in my personality, way of life, and ambitions and desires, and achievements.

I am seldom depressed to the extent that I am lifeless and feel that everything is futile. I make more decisions and with less frustration. In general I am happier—I take better care of the children. I have more insight into my own personality and others. I am more efficient at work. I am more aggressive.

I have rid myself of the greatest inferiority complex possible. I feel I am now a fairly attractive, competent person, who can handle the necessary crises of life that I will encounter. My fear of people in crowds and my fear of being alone have both been overcome almost entirely. I thoroughly enjoy people, my life, and those about me.

I am a great deal more self-sufficient, so that my relationships are not based merely on need, but I can now be a part of a reciprocal situation. I can assume much more responsibility for my own actions and thus am better able to act rather than just react. My anger at my family has subsided, and I no longer feel that they are to blame for my unhappiness in any present sense. Most importantly, I am able to feel joy and pain, which even with the latter is good, because *I'm* living, and not just something parasitic. I can trust another person enough to care, and to risk the consequences of the caring.

Greater Sense of Mastery

Responses classified under this heading probably overlap those to the question about changes in self-esteem. The ability to work out more effective solutions to life's problems, to tolerate adversity, including troublesome impulses and affects, and to cope with adult responsibilities is clearly an aspect of ego strength, which in turn is related to self-respect, self-esteem, and emotional maturity:

I have experienced a feeling of self confidence and also an ability to cope with my problems to a greater extent.

I am better able to conduct myself and my life in a nearly normal fashion. Have only occasional bouts with insomnia. Headaches somewhat improved. General relationships with other people improved.

Understanding of the causes of feelings of guilt and anxiety—disappearance of nightmares—feeling of confidence in ability to cope with own problems—high achievement and resultant sense of satisfaction, in areas previously blocked by anxieties.

Much better able to live my life as I please and better able to cope with life as it comes day to day. Feel freer to tell others what I think and where to get off!! Better able to live with fussy and "disturbed" parents.

The most important changes I have experienced is that when I get awfully depressed, instead of wanting to give up, I try to find out why I am depressed, and when I get tense, I try to do something to occupy myself. When I have aches and pains, I try not to worry about them and tell myself that I will be all right. I really try hard to help myself in every way that I can, instead of thinking as I used to, that I don't have anything to live for.

I can again cope with the responsibilities inherent in raising children. I can also hold a job without suffering tremendous doubts concerning my ability.

I have more calm and inner peace. I'm better able to cope with daily problems.

When the pressure is on and the feeling of anxiety comes, I am usually able to do some self-analysis and determine why. I understand myself better and know why I believe and feel the way I do about most things. I suppose the greatest thing I learned was to be myself and not try to be a perfectionist in everything.

After 6 months in therapy I obtained a driver's license. After the first year I moved into an apartment, bought a car, quit my job, moved to California and didn't like it, returned to my old job, bought another car and now live in my own place. I care for my son and handle my own affairs. I feel that I have matured quite a lot even though there is still room for improvement.

Here I must give an explanation. One of my problems before therapy was my inability to care about myself. It seems as though whenever I had someone else to care for or some responsibility to someone else, that I could handle problems okay. When it came to caring for myself, I just did not. Since I left therapy I have married and my wife is expecting a child shortly. This gives me a responsibility that I know I must not fail in. Although problems still exist, I run no more. I find myself thinking back to my therapy sessions and trying to use what I learned there. I try to determine why certain situations cause problems for me and then determine what is the best way to handle them. I do not let my problems pile up on me, I handle them as they come. I now realize that nothing is really as "earth shattering" as it may seem at the time, and after I have done all I can, I stand.

One interesting aspect of the patients' descriptions of changes which occurred with psychotherapy was their frequent mention of increased capacity to make sound judgments based on realistic appraisals of the facts at hand. Deficiencies in this regard were never mentioned specifically in the catalogue of initial complaints, while improvements in this regard were noted by fully 20 per cent of the total patient sample.

Other Changes

A number of additional changes attributed to the therapy experience, discernible from Figure 2, are illustrated in the following quotations.

I now tend to try and analyze some of the reasons and underlying motives behind my attitudes and behavior. I have accepted myself as a neurotic individual who has high anxiety and cumbersome defense mechanisms against it.

The most important change, I think, has been letting go of my own fantasies and facing my situation and experiences for what they are. I had always been a suspicious person, looking for someone to hurt my feelings, and then dwelling on it. Then, too, I'm able to find satisfaction and happiness in small ways that I had always overlooked before, probably because I was too busy worrying about myself. In many ways I'm an idealistic person, and perhaps the most important change in me has been learning the difference between things as they are and things as I think they should be.

Less depression.

Much less anxiety (almost none now), few pains in stomach and chest now, much better able to get along with other people and in social situations, able to sleep much better, and less tension.

I have accepted myself and live as a homosexual, being happy, contented, and productive in my work, which is very demanding. I do not fear relationships with others as much, am able to give and receive love, and have no more hallucinations or delusions. My family relationships are much improved and I never have suicidal or "escape" thoughts.

Have gained the knowledge and understanding of my fears to know that I am not alone, and the majority of them have no basis whatsoever.

As a final comment, the "illness" seemed very different to the patient at the end of therapy than it had at the beginning. Whether this change in outlook reflected "true" changes or merely an ability to talk differently about personal problems must remain an open question, but change apparently occurred, and patients became less inclined to stress the symptoms they experienced as most pressing when they entered therapy.

CURRENT ADJUSTMENT AND NEED
FOR FURTHER THERAPY

Follow-up studies of psychotherapy are rare, despite a few notable exceptions (e.g., Schjelderup 1955; Pfeffer 1959, 1961, 1963; Frank et al. 1963; Wallerstein 1968), and the average psychotherapist does not hear from former patients except when they are in need of further therapy. Indeed, many of them seem to avoid contacts with their former therapist, particularly if they manage well. In turn, while the therapist may be curious about his patients' lives following therapy, he refrains from getting in touch with them, and for good reasons. (One of the difficulties in carrying out follow-up studies on private patients is that the inquiry obviously must come from the therapist, who, for ethical reasons, is not at liberty to divulge his patients' names to an independent researcher.) No news is usually good news, but it is also possible that the former patient may have sought further help elsewhere.

Our data showed that 70 to 80 per cent of the sample were getting along at least reasonably well and were coping fairly adequately with their problems.

76. *On the whole how well do you feel you are getting along now?*

	N	%
Extremely well	13	11
Very well	32	26
Fairly well	53	43
Neither well nor poorly	10	8

Fairly poorly	4	3
Very poorly	6	5
Extremely poorly	2	2
[No response]	[2]	[2]

78. *How adequately do you feel you are dealing with any present problems?*

	N	%
Very adequately	19	16
Fairly adequately	66	54
Neither adequately nor inadequately	12	10
Somewhat inadequately	13	11
Very inadequately	6	5
[No response]	[3]	[3]
[No response: present problems]	[3]	[2]

On the other hand, 43 per cent of the respondents reported that they could use more therapy or felt in need of more (Item 16).

16. *How much in need of further therapy do you feel now?*

	N	%
No need at all	22	18
Slight need	45	37
Could use more	31	25
Considerable need	15	12
Very great need	7	6
[No response]	[2]	[2]

The percentage of patients who actually sought therapy at a later date (23 per cent) is perhaps a better indicator of "need." It should also be pointed out that therapy was often discontinued because the therapist completed his residency training or was transferred to another service. The therapy of a sizable number of patients was stopped in midstream, as it were, which may account for the relatively frequent expression of need for further therapy. The general tenor of the spontaneous comments accompanying the responses suggested that those who felt that further therapy was desirable did not consider it crucial.

Some people commented on the discomfort engendered by the questionnaire itself. One person said: "In thinking about it all again I longed to see my therapist once more, but I realize that he has done all he can for me and that now it is up to me."

Figure 3 compares patients' reports of presenting symptoms at the time of entering therapy* and difficulties reported as still existing at the time of answering the questionnaire. On the whole, patients described themselves as markedly improved, and a general diminution of symptoms seemed to have occurred. However, as previously noted, sensitivity to problems in interpersonal relationships increased.

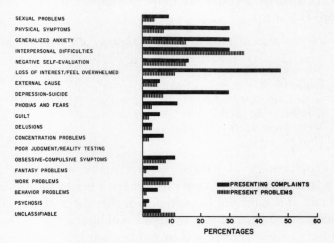

Figure 3

CORRELATES OF THERAPEUTIC CHANGE

We shall next turn to a consideration of the relationships between the amount of therapeutic change which the pa-

* These symptoms are listed in Figures 1 and 2 and they are repeated here to facilitate comparisons.

tient describes (Cluster P2) and other attitudes expressed in the questionnaire. This analysis was intended to explore patient attitudes which may have systematic relationships to their assessment of therapeutic change. Table 4 presents selected coefficients of correlation.

Table 4. Selected Correlates of Amount of Therapeutic Change (Cluster P2)

Variable		r
Cluster P1:	Therapist's warmth	.32**
Cluster P3:	Present adjustment	.42**
Cluster P4:	Amount of change apparent to others	.62**
Cluster P5:	Therapist's respect and interest	.50**
Cluster P9:	Degree of disturbance before therapy	.18*
Cluster P10:	Experience/activity level	.52**
Item P34:	I often felt I was "just another patient."	—.33**
Item P35:	The therapist was always keenly attentive.	.37**
Item P40:	I feel that he often didn't understand my real feelings.	—.33**
Item P76:	How well do you feel you are getting along now?	.50**
Item P80:	How soon after entering therapy did you feel any marked change?	—.60**

* P < .05.
** P < .01.

It seems evident that the amount of improvement noted by a patient in psychotherapy is highly correlated with his attitudes toward the therapist. Broken limbs can be properly set by a physician whom one does not know or even one toward whom one has considerable antipathy. However, it is most unlikely that successful psychotherapy can occur under such conditions. Indeed, psychotherapy was seen by our respondents as an intensely personal experience. More important, the therapist's warmth, his respect and interest, and his perceived competence and activity emerged as important ingredients in the amount of change reported by the patient. The more uncertain the patient felt about the therapist's attitude toward him, the less change he tended to experience.

Amount of therapeutic change, not unexpectedly, was associated appreciably with present adjustment but bore little relationship to the degree of disturbance reported before therapy began. Also, the amount of change was greatest when it was perceived as occurring soon after the beginning of therapy and as having been apparent to others.

Therapist's Warmth and Therapist's Interest, Integrity, and Respect

Since these two clusters of responses showed a relatively high degree of overlap ($r = .55$) and thus apparently measured related attitudes, it seemed advisable to compare some of the correlations (Table 5).

It is noteworthy that while the patient's assessment of both the therapist's warmth and his interest and respect correlated substantially with the amount of therapeutic change, the coefficients are of moderate size, suggesting that other factors may have been of equal and perhaps greater importance in determining the therapeutic outcome. This finding departs somewhat from the earlier study (Strupp, Wallach, and Wogan 1964), in which over-riding importance was attributed to the patient's attitudes toward the therapist. However, since the present coefficients are based on a considerably larger number of cases, they probably have greater stability and may be a better estimate of the true relationship among the variables.

The key to the Warmth cluster is found in Item 48: "I felt there usually was a good deal of warmth in the way he talked to me." Concomitant with this assertion, most respondents denied that the therapist's attitude was cold and distant, nor was the tone of his statements experienced as cold, stiff, and formal.

Turning to the Interest, Integrity, and Respect Cluster, key responses were 33 ("I feel the therapist was genuinely

Table 5. Selected Correlates of Therapist's Warmth (Cluster P1) and Therapist's Interest, Integrity, and Respect (Cluster P5)

Variable	Cluster P1	Cluster P5
	r	r
Item P30: There were times when I experienced intense anger toward my therapist.	−.22*	
Item P34: I often felt I was "just another patient."	−.42**	−.60**
Item P35: The therapist was always keenly attentive.	.33**	.59**
Item P36: The therapist often used very abstract language.	−.25**	−.30**
Item P37: He very rarely engaged in small talk	−.36**	
Item P39: The therapist's manner was quite natural and unstudied.	.52**	.46**
Item P40: I feel that he often didn't understand my real feelings.	−.34**	−.41**
Item P41: I feel he was extremely passive.	−.46**	−.38**
Item P44: Nothing the therapist said or did ever decreased my self-respect.	.23**	.24**
Item P50: The tone of his statements tended to be rather neutral.	−.24**	−.18*
Item P57: I was almost never given any direct reassurances by the therapist.	−.35**	−.28**
Item P58: I had the feeling the therapist sometimes criticized things I did or said.	−.19*	−.31**
Item P59: The therapist showed very little interest in my dreams and fantasies.		−.21*
Item P62: I was often uncertain about the therapist's real feelings toward me.	−.40**	−.48**

* $P < .05$.
** $P < .01$.

interested in helping me") and 47 ("I had a feeling of absolute trust in the therapist's integrity as a person"). Other relevant statements in the cluster included feelings of being respected as a person, of being fully accepted by the therapist, of having a firm conviction about the therapist's interest in helping, and of being treated as a worthwhile person.

A "good" therapist was seen as always keenly attentive, willing to engage in small talk, having a manner that patients experienced as natural and unstudied, saying or doing nothing that decreased the patient's self-respect, at times giving direct reassurance, never criticizing, and leaving no doubt about his "real" feelings. By contrast,* the following characteristics were seen as incompatible with the "ideal" therapist: causing (or allowing) the patient to experience intense anger toward him; making him feel "just another patient"; using abstract language (which, presumably, the patient does not understand); failing to understand his "real" feelings; passivity (admittedly a very vague phrase but apparently interpreted by the respondents to mean being unresponsive and "doing nothing"); and being "neutral" (evidently interpreted as an indication of lack of interest and concern).

The therapist characterized here is in important respects both similar to and different from the stereotype of the psychoanalyst. To be sure, the typical therapist emerged as a benign, interested, accepting, and attentive professional who had the patient's interest at heart and who was keenly interested in working with him. But, contrary to the stereotype of impersonality, he was viewed as a practitioner who was actively engaged in a real (as opposed to an "as-if") relationship with his patients. He was not averse to occasionally giving assurance and direct advice; he was friendly, warm, and not detached; and he seemed to keep close to the patient's everyday reality. It is quite clear that he did not encourage the expression of negative feelings or dependency wishes; he dealt firmly with the patient as an adult and helped him work through problems in his daily life. A "good" therapist, as the patients saw him, did not stimulate

* The converse of the various coefficients reported in Table 5 of course supports these statements in the same manner.

angry feelings nor did he assume an impersonal role; instead, he actively participated in the verbal exchange, kept the patient "moving," and pointed out constructive modes of behavior.

Whether this role was a function of the relative inexperience and tendency to "play it by ear" of the therapists in our survey or whether the approach was deliberate we are, of course, unable to say. It is quite possible that the therapist acted "naturally" not because he had been trained in this therapeutic technique but because he was following a common-sense approach. Nor can we make any assertions about the degree of skill displayed by a given therapist in a particular instance. However, the data support the view that therapists who did not behave in the manner described were less highly esteemed and that their patients reported fewer favorable changes. Stated differently, the "natural" approach made sense to the patient, whereas other approaches did not. The data shed no light on the question of whether the therapeutic approach varied with the patient, although such data might be desirable.

It was somewhat remarkable that our data indicated that negative transference feelings did not occur with any frequency. A number of factors, singly or in combination, seem to have kept them to a minimum. The first concern in most forms of therapy is to build a positive working relationship, which is essential to therapeutic change. Furthermore, such a relationship serves as a counterbalance to negative feelings, which always must be dealt with in psychotherapy, even if they are driven underground. A patient who harbors strong hostility toward authority figures, for example, is very likely to transfer such hostility to a therapist who remains a fairly shadowy figure, and most therapists in our sample, perhaps unwittingly, counteracted such feelings by quickly establishing a well-defined relationship with their patients.

Apart from the therapist's behavior as a clearly delineated reality figure, the following factors were probably responsible: relatively infrequent sessions, the face-to-face position in the interview, early (perhaps premature) transference interpretations, and emphasis on day-to-day events as opposed to fantasies.

Further data on the patients' views of their therapists were gathered through responses to an open-ended item (Item 81). These responses were categorized by means of the scheme described in Appendix G and fell into two major areas: attitudes toward the therapist and characteristics attributed to the therapist. Included in the first category were statements of trust, confidence, and respect, attitudes of liking and friendship, and expressions of gratitude and appreciation of their opposites. Prominent among the personality characteristics mentioned were capability, intelligence, warmth, acceptance, interest, kindness, and patience.

A more detailed presentation of these results may be found in Appendix G. In general, favorable comments far outweighed negative ones, whether the patient was describing his attitude toward the therapist or what he assumed to be the therapist's attitude toward him.

Length, Frequency, and Intensity of Experience

Table 6 provides some insight into attitudes and responses related to the length, frequency, and intensity of the therapy.

It may therefore be asserted that, as far as this investigation is concerned, the length of treatment, its relative frequency, and the intensity of the emotional experience, *as reported and judged by the patient*, had no bearing on outcome, irrespective of whether the patient's report or more objective criteria were used. Indeed, more frequent sessions had a somewhat *negative* correlation with the amount of change. And—to anticipate subsequent comparisons per-

Table 6. *Selected Correlates of Length of Therapy, Frequency of Sessions, and Intensity of Emotional Experience (Cluster P7)*

	Variable	With Specified Therapist		
		Length	Frequency	Intensity of Emotion
		r	r	r
Cluster P2:	Amount of change		−.20*	
Cluster P5:	Therapist's interest, integrity, respect		−.19*	
Cluster P10:	Experience/activity		−.27**	.24**
Item P30:	There were times when I experienced intense anger toward my therapist.	.29**		
Item P36:	The therapist often used very abstract language.			−.18*
Item P41:	I feel he was extremely passive.		.18*	
Item P44:	Nothing the therapist said or did ever decreased my self-respect.		−.19*	
Item P51:	I was never given any instructions or advice on how to conduct my life.		.27**	
Item P52:	The therapist often talked about psychoanalytic theory.			.19*
Item P53:	A major emphasis was upon my attitudes and feelings about the therapist.	.30**		
Item P55:	A major emphasis was upon childhood experiences.	.34**		
Item P57:	I was almost never given any direct reassurances by the therapist.		.22*	−.20*
Item P59:	My therapist showed very little interest in my dreams and fantasies.	−.19*		
Item P67:	How well did you feel you were getting along at the beginning of therapy?	−.27*		
Item P68:	How long before entering therapy did you feel in need of professional help?			−.18*
Item P80:	How soon after entering therapy did you feel any marked change?		.22*	

* $P < .05$.
** $P < .01$.

84

CHAPTER 5

taining to objective measures of therapeutic results—none
of the variables under discussion seemed to play a part in
the therapeutic outcome.

ARE THERAPEUTIC CHANGES APPARENT TO OTHERS?

Patients were asked to estimate the extent of change
which they felt had been apparent to people closest to them
—close friends, co-workers, acquaintances, and the like.
There was a slight tendency for the greatest amount of
change to have been apparent to persons closest to the patient. Not unexpectedly, change apparent to others was
closely associated with over-all change, current adjustment,
and the rapidity with which change took place (Table 7).

Table 7. *Selected Correlates of Amount of Change Apparent to Others (Cluster P4)*

Variable		r
Cluster P2:	Amount of change	.62**
Cluster P3:	Present adjustment/current status	.37**
Cluster P5:	Therapist's interest, integrity, respect	.19*
Cluster P9:	Degree of disturbance before therapy	.18*
Cluster P10:	Experience/activity level	.34**
Item P11:	Total number of hours with major therapist	.18*
Item P76:	How well do you feel you are getting along now?	.50**
Item P80:	How soon after entering therapy did you feel any marked change?	−.50**
Item FD20:	Degree of symptomatic improvement	.21*

* $P < .05$.
** $P < .01$.

SOCIOENVIRONMENTAL VARIABLES

We shall have more to say about relationships to objective data on outcomes, but for the present it suffices to note
that patient's reports were essentially independent of the
socioenvironmental variables under discussion. None of the
variables investigated (age, sex, family income, and occupa-

tion/education) showed statistically significant correlations with the attitude clusters isolated from the patient questionnaire. While individual items correlated significantly with the variables in questions, the coefficients for the most part were quite low and may well be due to chance.

6.

OTHER VIEWPOINTS

The previous chapter dealt with the patient's assessment of his therapy experiences and those attitudes which seemed to be associated, in his view at least, with the quality of the outcome. In this chapter we shall consider assessments of outcome based on initial diagnostic impressions by the clinic staff, therapists' progress notes, and final case summaries. Our purpose is to study variables which might have a bearing on the clinic's (and indirectly the therapist's) initial appraisal and ratings of therapy outcome. An additional aim of this chapter is to explore the relationship between the patient's and the clinic's assessment of the therapeutic experience.

It will be recalled that clinical evaluations based on the therapist's notes and summaries were quantified by trained raters. The interrelationships of these evaluations are presented in Table 8. It may be seen that ratings of over-all success are, for the most part, identical with ratings of symptomatic improvement; however, the remaining variables were neither very highly interrelated nor associated with over-all success. The over-all success rating was re-

Table 8. *Interrelationships among Clinical Evaluations*

Variable	FD16	FD17	FD18	Item FD19	FD20	FD21
Item FD16: Amount of subjective discomfort		.44**				
Item FD17: Degree of impairment			−.21*	−.29**	−.22*	−.18*
Item FD18: Patient's motivation for therapy				.40**	.42**	.43**
Item FD19: Prognosis					.36**	.24**
Item FD20: Degree of symptomatic improvement						.77**
Item FD21: Over-all success						

* $P < .05$.
** $P < .01$.

garded as the most reliable and objective estimate of therapeutic outcome which was available to us. It is noteworthy that neither the amount of initial discomfort nor the degree of impairment were highly correlated with this outcome measure.

Some Correlates of Success

Table 9 shows that few *objective* variables were systematically related to clinical evaluations of success or of symptomatic improvement. Moreover, since a great many correlation coefficients were computed, the relatively small number of significant ones may well be due to chance. However, the relationships do parallel each other, and thus may deserve greater credence. Three findings should be noted: (1) Older patients (who were also more likely to have a larger number of children) tended to achieve greater therapeutic success. It is probable that this result is a function of greater persistence in keeping appointments and

Table 9. Selected Correlates of Clinical Evaluations with File Data at Beginning of Therapy

Variable		Symptom Improvement	Over-All Success
Item FD3:	Age	.30**	.25**
Item FD6:	Number of children	.22*	.30**
Item FD13a:	Previous hospitalizations		
Item FD13b:	Number and length of hospitalizations		
Item FD15:	How long had symptoms been present	−.29**	−.19*
Item FD29:	Distance traveled to clinic		
Item FD40:	Canceled interviews	−.21*	−.24*

* P < .05.
** P < .01.

"seeing it through" (see [3]). (2) The more chronic the patient's condition, the less likely was therapy to be crowned with success. However, neither the number or length of previous psychiatric hospitalizations was related to the success ratings. (3) Finally, the more successful patients tended to have fewer canceled interviews.

On the whole, the foregoing results are unremarkable. What they do suggest is that therapeutic success must be a function of other factors.

PATIENTS' AND CLINIC'S VIEW OF EACH OTHER

The groundwork has now been laid for discussing the degree of convergence between the patient's and the clinic's view of the therapy experience. At the same time, we shall look for reliable predictors of therapy outcomes.

Therapeutic Outcome

Table 10 presents the statistical relationships between the patients' reports and assessments based on information from the clinic charts.

Perhaps of greatest interest is the association of the amount of therapeutic change the patient described (Cluster

Table 10. Selected Relationships between Patients' Reports and Therapists' Judgments of Outcome

Patients' Reports		FD20: Symptom Improvement	FD21: Over-All Success
Item P39:	The therapist's manner was quite natural and unstudied.	.22*	.20*
Item P71:	How great was the internal "pressure" at the beginning?	.21*	.22*
Item P76:	How well do you feel you are getting along now?	.24**	.20*
Item P80:	How soon after entering therapy did you feel any marked change?	−.39**	−.23*
Cluster P2:	Amount of change	.36**	.23**
Cluster P4:	Change apparent to others	.21*	

* $P < .05$.
** $P < .01$.

P2) and the therapist's evaluation of the treatment in his closing summary, which served as the basis for the ratings of symptomatic improvement (Item FD20) and over-all success (Item FD21). While correlations of .36 and .23 are only moderate, they are consonant with the coefficient of .36 reported in the previous investigation (Strupp, Wallach, and Wogan 1964) for over-all success as rated retrospectively by the therapist. In view of the unreliability inherent in investigations of this kind, it is encouraging to note this moderate consensus. While therapists and patients clearly shared certain notions of the quality of the therapeutic outcome, they judged it from different vantage points. As noted earlier, patients generally tended to be more enthusiastic in their assessments than the therapists.

In the majority of instances the correlations of symptom improvement and over-all success paralleled each other, which was of course predictable from their high intercorrelation. Although most of the coefficients reported in Table 10 are low, we may note a number of consistent relationships. (1) Success was greatest when the therapist's manner was perceived as natural; (2) patients who felt under the greatest internal pressure (motivation) at the beginning of therapy tended to have the most successful outcomes; (3) successful patients tended to report that they were getting along better at the time of the survey, suggesting that the therapeutic results were durable; (4) successful patients tended to experience marked changes most rapidly (the negative sign of the coefficients is accounted for by the fact that rapid changes received a lower numerical score). On the whole, the conclusion seems justified that patients whose therapy was rated successful (as well as those rated as failures) tended to see themselves as such; therapeutic change, where it occurred, was perceived as having taken place fairly rapidly once treatment was undertaken and seemed to be lasting.

In order to explore further the association between ratings of therapeutic outcome (Item FD21) and individual questionnaire items, chi square analyses were undertaken. Whereas correlation coefficients indicate the magnitude of a relationship, they may in certain cases yield less information than the chi square method, which as a nonparametric measure may be more suitable. However, it will be noted that for the most part the results are similar (Appendix H).

1. Patients whose therapy was judged successful by the clinic were significantly less likely to have had additional psychotherapy following termination than patients whose success was rated low.

2. Such patients reported considerably less need for further therapy at the time of answering the questionnaire than patients rated as relative therapeutic failures.

3. Such patients expressed themselves as more satisfied with the outcome of their therapy than others. No patient in this group described himself as dissatisfied with his psychotherapy experience at the clinic, and an appreciable number (fifteen) rated themselves as "highly satisfied" de-

spite the fact that the clinic regarded their success as mini-
mal. To some extent patients may have reported what they
believed the clinic wanted to hear, but it is equally likely
that *subjective* changes and *subjective* gains were greater
than the clinic evaluators appreciated.

FILE DATA SUCCESS RATING COMPARED
WITH QUESTIONNAIRE ITEM II

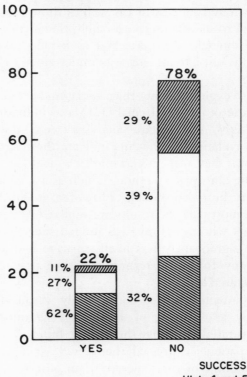

Figure 4

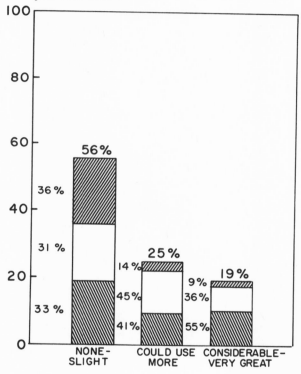

FILE DATA SUCCESS RATING COMPARED
WITH QUESTIONNAIRE ITEM 16

"How much in need of further therapy do you feel now ?"

SUCCESS
High   4 and 5
Moderate 3
Low   1 and 2

Figure 5

4. Similarly, patients rated successful believed themselves to be getting along better at the time of answering the questionnaire than failure cases. While this association is statistically significant, an appreciable number of patients

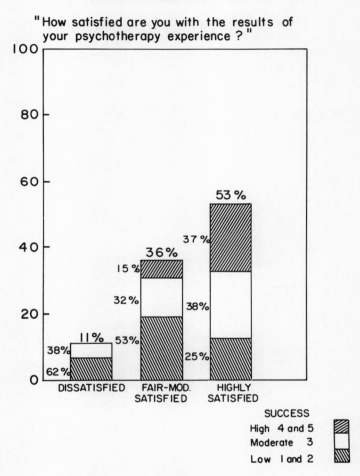

Figure 6

in the latter group (fourteen) reported getting along very well, whereas only one success patient stated that he was getting along poorly. Figures 4–7 present these relationships.

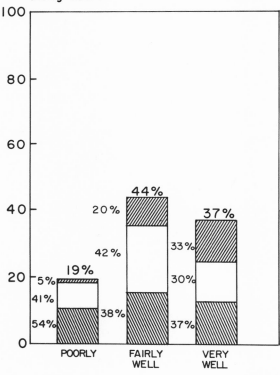

FILE DATA SUCCESS RATING COMPARED
WITH QUESTIONNAIRE ITEM 76

"How well do you feel you are getting
     along now ?"

SUCCESS

High   4 and 5
Moderate   3
Low   1 and 2

Figure 7

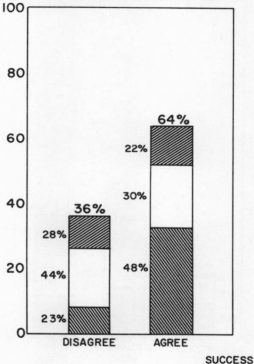

FILE DATA SUCCESS RATING COMPARED
WITH QUESTIONNAIRE ITEM 30

"There were times I experienced
intense anger toward my therapist."

Figure 8

Finally, the items unrelated to success as measured by the
clinic are of interest. This category includes adjustment at
the time of entering therapy, initial degree of disturbance,
chronicity of disturbance, initial level of anxiety, and degree of symptom change following therapy. The widely

FILE DATA SUCCESS RATING COMPARED
WITH QUESTIONNAIRE ITEM 39

"Therapist's manner was quite natural
and unstudied."

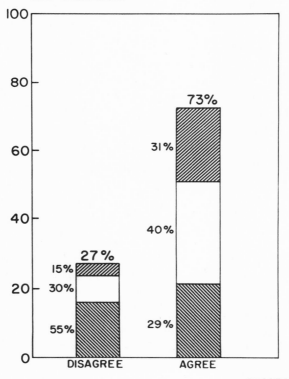

Figure 9

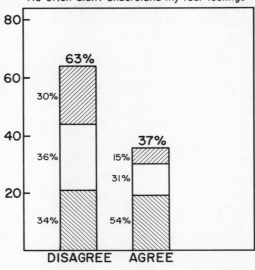

FILE DATA SUCCESS RATING COMPARED
WITH QUESTIONNAIRE ITEM 40
"He often didn't understand my real feelings"

Figure 10

divergent standards used by the patients in their evaluations may well have caused these inconclusive results.

Therapist's Attitudes and Therapeutic Climate

To pursue the relationship between success and patients' reports of the therapist's attitudes, we shall discuss the five items which showed a statistically significant association (chi square) with rated success (see Appendix I and Figs. 8–12). (1) Patients whose therapy was rated as successful were less likely to have felt intense anger at the therapist than failure cases. (2) They tended to rate the

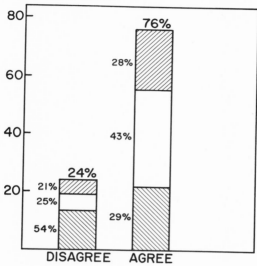

FILE DATA SUCCESS RATING COMPARED
WITH QUESTIONNAIRE ITEM 48
"Usually a good deal of warmth in the way he talked to me"

Figure 11

therapist's manner as natural and unstudied. A large group (in this instance 73 per cent) answered this question in the affirmative irrespective of whether they were rated as successes or failures. (3) Probably as part of their general dissatisfaction with therapy, failure cases were more likely to complain that the therapist often did not understand their real feelings. (4) Patients rated as successful showed a greater tendency to credit the therapist with a good deal of warmth than did failures. (5) A larger proportion of successes than failures considered themselves fully accepted

FILE DATA SUCCESS RATING COMPARED
WITH QUESTIONNAIRE ITEM 60

"I usually felt I was fully accepted by
the therapist "

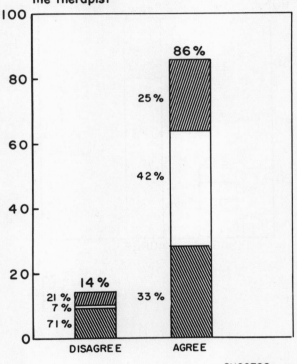

Figure 12

by the therapist.

It should be kept in mind that a patient who made favorable statements about his therapist did not necessarily have a successful outcome; however, a patient who made unfavorable comments about his therapist was usually a member of the low success group. Thus the therapist's warmth, acceptance, and naturalness were not a guarantee of therapeutic success or a necessary and sufficient condition for a good therapeutic outcome, but lack of these traits was a fairly reliable predictor of a poor therapeutic outcome.

From the patient's point of view, a warm, accepting, and understanding therapist was desirable but not essential; a therapist who, in the patient's eyes, was definitely deficient in these areas was more apt to fail. The data also showed that a respondent usually subscribed to positive statements about his former therapist unless he had strong feelings to the contrary. In the former case, the attributed qualities may have been stereotypic; however, when a patient expressed himself negatively about his therapist, internal evidence from the data supports the conclusion that he usually meant it.

We may conclude that as long as the therapist maintains an attitude of benevolent neutrality and genuine interest, an important prerequisite for successful psychotherapy has been met. This given, the relative success of therapy is then a function of other factors, such as the extent and character of the patient's emotional disturbance, his motivation for therapy and—last but perhaps not least—the therapist's technical skill in dealing with his problems. The attitudinal component of the therapist's behavior definitely plays a part, but it is probably not decisive.

7.

A CLOSER LOOK AT FAILURES

Since a large majority of our respondents regarded their psychotherapy as a worthwhile experience, it is natural to wonder about those patients whose responses were less favorable. Is it possible to find specific reasons for their disillusionment, and can their evaluations teach us something about poor outcomes in general? In order to explore these questions, we chose twenty failure cases for closer scrutiny. Patients in this sample included persons who expressed dissatisfaction with the results of their treatment, claimed they had experienced little if any symptom improvement, and asserted that their over-all benefit from psychotherapy was negligible.

In approaching this problem we must recognize that the individuals who expressed dissatisfaction with their therapy were not necessarily therapeutic failures by other criteria, but it would be difficult to take issue with their felt disappointment in the value of psychotherapy. A self-evaluation is an index in its own right. Whether it should be taken at face value is, of course, another matter. As pointed out in Chapter 6, there was a significant relationship between the patients' subjective ratings of the degree of therapeutic success and ratings based on the clinic charts. Similarly, patients who described themselves as therapeutic failures were judged to have been less well motivated at the beginning of treatment, were thought to have shown less symptomatic improvement, and were rated lower in over-all success than those who described themselves as highly satisfied with the results of their therapy. In several essential respects, then, lack of success as rated by the patient paralleled the therapist's evaluation.

It should be kept in mind that the survey sample was composed of individuals who gave therapy a reasonable trial (a minimum of 25 hours). Such persons, therefore, probably differ from patients who dropped out after only a few interviews. Numerous studies have reported a drop-out rate of as high as 50 to 60 per cent after only one interview. Clearly, we are not dealing with such individuals, who cannot be said to have been "in therapy."

The sample of failure cases was compared with the total sample in terms of biographical and therapeutic variables. The results are presented in Table 11. The therapeutic conditions were about the same for both groups: that is, they were all treated by therapists in training who moved from service to service and who had relatively little experience. As can be seen from the table, there was a range of variations among the patients themselves, however, and we shall comment on those which appear to have practical importance.

AGE, EDUCATION, MARITAL STATUS, AND DEGREE OF DISTURBANCE

It may be seen that the failure cases on the whole were younger, better educated, and more likely to be single than

Table 11. Clinic Chart Ratings of Failures and of Total Sample at Beginning of Therapy

Variable	Failure Cases (N = 20)		Total Sample (N = 122)	
	Frequency	%	Frequency	%
Sex				
Male	10	50	49	40
Female	10	50	73	60
Age				
18–25	12	60	55	45
26–33	5	25	37	30
34–41	2	10	21	17
42–49	1	5	8	7
50–	0	—	1	1
Marital status*				
Single	12	60	56	46
Married	6	30	56	46
Divorced	1	5	7	6
Widowed	1	5	3	2
Education				
Less than high school	1	5	14	12
High school graduate	3	15	27	22
Some college	9	45	57	47
College graduate	3	15	11	9
Graduate study	4	20	13	11
Occupation				
Student	13	65	53	43
Housewife	3	15	27	22
Unemployed	1	5	12	10
Other	3	15	30	25
Hours of therapy				
25–50	13	65	54	44
50–75	3	15	26	21
75–100	1	5	14	12
100–125	—	—	10	8
125–150	2	10	5	4
150+	1	5	8	7
Unknown	—	—	5	4
Type of therapist**				
Psychiatry resident	13	65	101	83
Psychology student	6	30	16	13
Staff psychiatrist	—	—	1	1
Staff psychologist	1	5	4	3
Prior hospitalization**				
Yes	4	20	48	39
No	16	80	59	48
Unknown	0	—	15	13

* Chi square significant .10.
** Chi square significant .02.

the average patient in our sample. Many were students at the time of treatment, their treatment tended to be shorter, and they had a lower incidence of prior hospitalizations than the average. We found no evidence that at the beginning of therapy they were regarded as more disturbed than either the success cases or the total sample. Comparisons of diagnoses and presenting symptoms were also inconclusive.

The young college student who is not too disturbed is often considered an ideal candidate for psychotherapy, yet we found this group to be over-represented among the failure cases: the trends indicated in Table 11 thus appear to be somewhat at variance with the usual assumptions about a "good" therapeutic patient. College students were eagerly sought by our young therapists as patients. However, in this sample older patients tended to achieve greater therapeutic success and had more hours in treatment. Apparently, older—and, one presumes, more mature—persons had a stronger desire both to obtain treatment and to continue it once they were accepted. They tended to be more reliable in keeping appointments and in seeing the treatment through to completion.

Students, by the very nature of their status in life, are unsettled vocationally, emotionally, and geographically and are truly a mobile group. The typical student in the failure sample had no family responsibilities and was not yet firmly committed to a career. The presence of such responsibilities may be of considerable importance in providing the sustained motivation which is crucial for prolonged self-scrutiny, and in some measure they are themselves a reflection of the patient's prior achievements in adult living. It is uncertain, of course, whether the students' emotional problems delayed marriage or a career choice, but there is a good chance that they did.

THERAPISTS' PROFESSIONAL AFFILIATION

A rather puzzling finding was that a greater percentage of the therapists of failure cases (30 per cent) were psychology students than was true for the total sample (13 per cent). The reasons for this discrepancy are obscure, and the number of cases involved is too small to draw definite conclusions. One possible factor may be that the psychology student is often very close in age to the student-patient and is involved in many of the same life issues. Psychiatric residents, on the other hand, are generally five to six years older than the average psychology trainee. Perhaps too much similarity creates difficulties for both parties. Some therapists remarked on the difficulty of maintaining proper perspective with a patient only one or two years their junior. One of the patients commented, "It was hard for me to think of him as an expert. He seemed scarcely older than I was." This was, in fact, the case. Another possible explanation is that psychology students may be too ready to accept students as good therapy risks without giving sufficient weight to the restrictions imposed by both their individual personalities and their current life situations.

In order to gain a better understanding of the factors leading to therapeutic failure, we studied the therapists' progress notes. Specifically, we looked at these records as therapists evaluating a therapeutic interaction. In doing so we were fully aware of the potential pitfalls of such an undertaking, including the temptation to second-guess the therapist in the light of subsequent developments. Nonetheless, our aim was not to denigrate the therapist but to gain insight into factors that might consistently make for failure. The trends which seemed most significant are discussed below.

PREMATURE TERMINATION

A common occurrence among the failure cases was premature termination of therapy for external reasons which could not be directly attributed to difficulties in the therapist-patient relationship. Admittedly, in many cases therapy was terminated because the therapist, the patient, or both were leaving: students graduated, wives terminated because their husbands changed jobs, therapists were transferred to another service or completed their training, etc. While such external reasons sometimes seemed a convenient excuse for terminating an unrewarding situation, premature termination was a factor in twelve of the twenty failure cases. The following therapist's report is illustrative of such a termination, as well as of the frustrations which often result from an unfinished task.

This patient, a young man, sought treatment for the first time as a college student for anxiety, difficulties with studies, poor heterosexual relationships, and fears of being a homosexual. He was accepted for treatment immediately on a once-a-week basis by a second-year resident. He canceled appointments occasionally and had a total of 30 hours of treatment before he graduated from college. During treatment he seemed to the therapist to be quite passively resistant, as manifested by "prolonged periods of silence and inability to verbalize the hostility and fears toward authority figures." At the end of treatment the therapist felt that the patient was somewhat less inhibited and more aware of the nature of his problems.

Four years later this patient participated in our research project. He was now in a large northern city where he lived alone and worked as a cartographer. He did not feel that he had benefited from his therapy, was extremely dissatisfied with its outcome, and denied having changed as a result of treatment:

I have experienced a few changes, both positive and negative, since leaving psychotherapy, but I do not believe the changes resulted from the psychotherapy experience. In the four years since psychotherapy, I have proven to myself that I can make it on my own, financially at least; and this has given me a measure of self-confidence. My job brings me into contact with many people, and I have learned to be less self-conscious and more at ease in dealing with people. On the other hand, I have made no progress socially. Four more years of anxieties and frustrations concerning my original symptoms have added bitterness, sadness, and a growing feeling of hopelessness to an already pessimistic outlook on life.

Neither this report nor the therapist's notes enable us to pinpoint the reasons for the patient's negative appraisal, but unquestionably therapy was terminated prematurely. It was known from the beginning of treatment that the patient was a senior in college and that he would be leaving the vicinity within a few months. Therefore, there was a particular need for the therapist to set realistic goals which had some prospect of being achieved within the available time and to communicate the exigencies of the situation to the patient. As was often true in the failure group, there was no indication that this had been done. Therapy apparently proceeded as if it were timeless, with a rather vague idea that treatment would be continued "somewhere else" after the patient left school.

As Bergin (1963) has shown, psychotherapy may benefit a patient but it may also create new problems. Care must be taken that the therapist not do so unwittingly. It would seem preferable to work on a limited range of problems, so as to leave the patient somewhat optimistic about future psychotherapy, than to strive for poorly defined, long-range goals which are patently unobtainable in the time available and thus to risk adding to his sense of failure and low self-esteem.

A related problem was observed when a patient was transferred to another therapist because his therapist was leaving the service. Unresolved feelings and attitudes toward the initial therapist were often transferred to his successor, and the affective overtones produced by such premature termination substantially influenced subsequent therapeutic encounters. Even in the absence of conflicting attitudes toward a former therapist, patients could not help but make comparisons between the present and the former therapist. Direct comparisons of this nature were often perceived by the neophyte therapist as a reflection on his own keenly felt lack of experience. His insecurity in the professional role often seemed to make him ineffective in handling such material. Then too, frequently patients made comparisons for individious purposes, sometimes unconsciously and sometimes quite consciously. The therapists' two most frequent responses to such maneuvers were either silence or direct interpretation of the patient's feelings toward the present therapist. Rarely were they handled in a manner that held some hope of resolving the patient's ambivalence toward his former therapist.

From the standpoint of clinic policy and training, it seems that the assignment of patients should be accomplished with an eye to the length of time for which treatment is possible. It must be stressed that if the patient is available for only a limited time, care must be taken to set circumscribed goals and to apprise the patient of these limitations. Similarly, if the therapist is available for a limited time, the therapeutic interaction should be structured accordingly. Unexpected transfer to another therapist is bound to create problems. Such transfers are often unavoidable, but if they are anticipated, the possible consequences should be carefully weighed in arriving at a realistic treatment plan. Perhaps student therapists who are assigned to a clinic for relatively short periods should be taught techniques of brief intervention and should be restricted to this type of approach whenever possible. In any case, the notion that "a little therapy won't hurt" is a myth which tends to be uncritically accepted by neophytes (and perhaps by their supervisors). All too often prematurely interrupted therapy leaves the patient not only unimproved but also disillusioned with the very source which might have offered him some help.

THERAPEUTIC RELATIONSHIP

Difficulties in the therapeutic relationship, which could be loosely labeled transference and countertransference problems, were apparent in fully three-quarters of the failure cases, as illustrated in the following report.

This patient was a 19-year-old woman with one child who was caught in an extremely stormy relationship with her student husband. Ostensibly, her marital difficulties were the basis of her request for treatment. She was seen by an inexperienced female therapist at weekly intervals for a total of 33 sessions. She admitted to "a certain amount of relief from anxiety" as a result of treatment and said that she would strongly recommend psychotherapy to a close friend with emotional problems. However, she described herself as rather dissatisfied with the results of her psychotherapy experience because "I felt we never really got to the root of my problems." The therapist seemed to agree with this impression and wrote in her closing summary: "Progress was completely absent in the short psychotherapy relationship. [The patient] had very little motivation to achieve insight into her personality characteristics, and the unstable relationship with her husband and mother appeared to impede progress."

Both therapist and patient said that treatment was terminated because the therapist was leaving town. This was true, but the patient had stopped keeping her appointments over two months prior to the therapist's scheduled departure, at a time when both parties agreed that treatment was still indicated. As far as could be determined from the therapist's progress notes, the course of treatment was marked by resistance, missed appointments, passive-aggressive maneuvers, and emotional outbursts by the patient.

As an adolescent, this young woman had been in treatment for two years with a very experienced child therapist, of whom she said, "He fantastically affected me." Her second therapist may well have been faced with some affective carryover from the initial treatment. The patient admitted that "I was constantly aware of therapist B's inexperience compared to my first therapist who was/is in my opinion one of the top psychotherapists in this country in his field. I was constantly aware of the difference in experience in B's sessions." She said of her second therapist, "I felt that she was very sympathetic but I tended to doubt whether she had a real grasp on my problems." In her eleventh session she reported the following dream to her therapist: "I dreamed that you called me and said that you weren't going to see me anymore, that my problem was more than you expected and that you couldn't help me."

The progress notes, of course, reveal less about the therapist than the patient, but some clues about the nature of the relationship emerged. The patient was said to be consistently remiss in keeping appointments and in paying for her clinic visits. After 4 months of treatment the therapist mentioned the fact that the patient had yet to make a payment or to make arrangements for payment. She then left it to the patient to decide whether she cared to discuss the matter! The patient changed the subject, and no further mention of the poor payment record was made. During treatment, the patient became pregnant, and when she mentioned this, her therapist responded that she too had just found out that she was also pregnant. The particularly unfortunate aspects of this revelation and the discussion that followed can be understood when it is noted that the patient was in the midst of an extremely hostile, dependent, and competitive relationship with her mother, and that a large part of her problem at the time of therapy centered around arguments with her mother concerning the care of her first child.

This woman would have been a difficult case under the best circumstances, but the therapist's apparent willingness to avoid necessary and important confrontations seems to have played a part in her lack of success. All of the patient's interpersonal relationships, including the therapeutic one, were stormy, and one may be permitted the speculation that both participants seized on the therapist's impending departure as a welcome release. It has been noted that the patient stopped therapy without a formal termination. According to her report, the therapist made no follow-up attempts and then closed the case after one month "because of this indication of extremely poor motivation." However, the reason given in the final case summary was the therapist's departure. Interestingly, the patient gave the same reason for termination in her questionnaire.

Inadequate handling of transference and countertransference problems appeared to be prominent in most therapeutic failures, although, as might be expected, it was not always specified, other "reasons" being more palatable to both therapist and patient. Nevertheless, the therapist's lack of tact and sensitivity, and perhaps sheer technical incompetence as well, appears to have been a major factor. Whether such shortcomings can be remedied by further training or whether they are inherent in the therapist's personality and relatively impervious to change is an open question. Truax and Carkhuff (1967), who have trained psychotherapists and have had extensive research experience, seem to feel that most inexperienced psychotherapists can be trained to become more understanding. This may well be true in many cases, but in our opinion such conclusions should not be accepted unquestioningly.

8.

INGREDIENTS OF SUCCESSFUL PSYCHOTHERAPY

In this chapter we compare the evaluation of therapeutic outcome made by the patient with that of the clinic. Our purpose is to determine the areas of agreement regarding the ingredients of a successful psychotherapeutic interaction, as well as the changes which patients believe to be most important and which withstood the test of their life experience after therapy ended.

CHARACTERISTICS OF THE PATIENT

On the basis of data from the clinic files we found the typical success patient to be somewhat older than the average in our survey, married, with children. He sought help rather promptly after recognizing that "something was wrong." He kept appointments more faithfully and appeared to be less incapacitated by his difficulties than the unsuccessful patient. He noted relatively rapid improvement once therapy got under way.

The motivation for psychotherapy seemed to be important in the eyes of both the clinic and the patients. As already noted, patients regarded by the clinic as having shown the greatest improvement had the fewest canceled appointments, which may be viewed as one index of motivation. Furthermore, such patients tended to describe themselves as being under great internal pressure to do something about their problems at the beginning of therapy. Finally, they reported feeling more disturbed at the time of their first clinic contact than did others.

These indices of motivation are admittedly imprecise and somewhat indirect. Nevertheless, there seemed to be agreement that the patient's own initiative, discomfort, and determination are crucial to the success of the therapeutic undertaking. Both therapists and patients appeared to believe that eagerness for help, willingness to work with another person on one's problems, ability to withstand the painful feelings that emerge in therapy, and a level of emotional maturity high enough to make the foregoing possible were among the keys to successful psychotherapy.

CHARACTERISTICS OF THE THERAPIST

The "Good" Therapist

A positive attitude toward the therapist proved to be closely related to success in therapy, irrespective of how that success was measured. Patients who rated their own therapy as successful described their therapists as warm, attentive, interested, understanding, and respectful. Furthermore, they perceived the therapist as experienced and active in the therapeutic situation. Patients rated highly successful by their therapists gave a similar description of the therapist. These patients were less likely to report intense anger toward their therapists than were their less successful counterparts, who also tended to report uncertainty about the therapist's attitude toward them.

The composite image of the "good therapist" drawn by our respondents is thus that of a keenly attentive, interested, benign, and concerned listener—a friend who is warm and natural, is not averse to giving direct advice, who speaks one's language, makes sense, and rarely arouses intense anger. This portrait contrasts with the stereotype of the impersonal analyst, whose stance is detached, who creates a vacuum into which negative as well as positive feelings can flow, and who maintains a neutral though benign role, more a shadowy figure than a "real" person.

The question naturally arises as to whether the therapist's attitudes and behavior, as recorded by the patient, were the product of inexperience or a calculated technique to achieve optimum results within the limitations of this form of therapy—once or twice a week over a period of a year or so. The patients' preference was clear: they found a "human" therapist helpful. In some sense, however, the problem is analogous to asking a child about his preference for a parent. For a child the "ideal" parent is not necessarily the person who best prepares him to accept the responsibilities of adulthood and to endure the frustrations and delays in gratification that life inevitably holds in store. As the patients described him, the successful therapist was clearly a helpful person, but whether some other approach, perhaps less immediately satisfying to the patient, might have accomplished as much or even more is of course a moot question. We do not subscribe to the view of psychotherapy as "the purchase of friendship" (Schofield 1964), although this is what many patients obviously wanted and, if their reports are taken at face value, to some extent received. Clearly, in this instance, as in certain others, the patient's reports cannot be accepted at face value. Their perceptions (mixed, perhaps, with idealizations) of the good therapist cannot be construed as recommendations for training or practice, except in a very general way.

At this point the question of possible differences in the patients' perceptions of their therapists in our two studies suggests itself. Several difficulties preclude meaningful comparisons. It will be recalled that the therapists who participated in the first study were considerably more experienced than those in the second and that a number of their patients received psychoanalysis. While numerous authors (for example, Gill 1954) have attempted to differentiate psychoanalysis from other forms of psychotherapy, such distinctions are difficult to make in practice. A further complication is that the same patient was sometimes seen in what appeared to be orthodox analysis during one phase of his therapy and in some modified form during another.

It was our impression, however, that there were no significant differences between the two studies in patients' descriptions of their therapists. Indeed, the similarities were impressive, which may, of course, partially reflect the lack of refinement of our measuring instrument. We may speculate, however, that the more detached role of the therapist in psychoanalysis requires considerably greater skill and experience than the "natural" way of relating exemplified in Study 2. To project neutrality without giving the patient a feeling of rejection is no small achievement. We may surmise that numerous therapists in the first study succeeded in this feat, as indicated by the finding that even when the therapist's attitude was described by the patient in terms of the analytic model he believed that it reflected interest, empathy, respect, and concern. The issue of whether or not a more neutral stance leads to better therapeutic results—perhaps in the "classical" sense of resolving the transference neurosis more effectively and ultimately assuring the patient of greater autonomy—is exceedingly complex and cannot be resolved on the basis of our data.

The Role of Clinical Experience

The therapists in the second study were relatively inexperienced, and yet they obtained results which appeared to be as impressive as those reported for patients treated by the more highly experienced clinicians in Study 1. There were no appreciable differences in outcome or quality of the therapeutic relationship; length of therapy or frequency of sessions had no measurable bearing on outcome; and differences in therapeutic competence, as judged by supervisors, were also inconclusive.

Lest one rashly conclude that the therapist's competence is of no consequence, however, the following points must be considered. We must not lose sight of the fact that assessment of success in the two studies was not directly comparable. In both investigations the measures were overall ratings without precise anchoring points. Thus it is possible, and perhaps quite likely, that a rating of success for a patient who had undergone prolonged and intensive therapy with an experienced therapist meant something very different from a comparable rating for a patient who had had 25 or 50 sessions with a resident and achieved symptom relief. The kinds of changes reported by these two hypothetical patients may appear to be very similar, and statistical comparisons of ratings do not disclose the differences. Meaningful comparisons are still possible, however. There is no reason to believe that the patients in Study 2 were less disturbed than their counterparts in the earlier study. The evidence is fairly conclusive that both groups were suffering from relatively severe emotional or characterological disturbances, few of which could be classed as transient or situational. In addition, the young therapist may make up in enthusiasm and infectious optimism what he lacks in experience and well-founded caution. Precisely because of his inexperience, he may communicate

confidence when a more guarded approach would seem
appropriate to his experienced colleague. Our data, of
course, permit no test of this hypothesis. Certainly it con-
tradicts both intuition and previous investigators' reports.
Perhaps the simplest explanation is the best; the vagueness
inherent in criterion measures such as questionnaires makes
it impossible to specify the association of therapist expertise
and therapeutic results.

It is doubtless apparent that we are unwilling here to
denigrate the claims of long-term, intensive psychotherapy, although our findings, if taken literally, would suggest such a position. Until therapeutic results can be more
stringently defined (which would involve more incisive
comparisons of a patient's status upon entering therapy
with that upon leaving it), such an inference would be
inappropriate. Iron-clad evidence is lacking, but we believe
that, when reliable criteria and measuring instruments are
adopted, the results of long-term therapy by an experienced therapist will prove to be clearly distinguishable
from short-term therapy by a relatively inexperienced
practitioner.

THE NATURE OF THERAPEUTIC CHANGE

We have commented at some length on the kinds of
changes patients reported as a result of psychotherapy.
Most noteworthy perhaps was the relatively minor emphasis on alleviation of the common neurotic symptoms, such
as anxiety, depression, and physical disturbances, and the
focus on improvement in the areas of interpersonal relations and self-esteem. The view of therapeutic change
taken by the people in our survey thus coincides with that
of all analytically oriented therapists: it is seen not in terms
of "symptom removal" but as occurring on a broad front
and affecting a broad spectrum of life experience.

The fact that this kind of change was the most readily perceived and most highly valued by these patients argues against a concept of psychotherapy as a technique for the removal of specific symptoms and highlights the all-pervasive character of personality change. Patients reported a new or modified orientation toward life in general and an altered self-image; they further asserted that the change was apparent to close associates and that it had occurred relatively rapidly once therapy got under way.

One of the striking accomplishments of psychotherapy with this population (as is probably the case with most patients) was the transformation of what seemed to be mysterious and mystifying symptoms into phenomena with explainable antecedents. The patient came to view his difficulties in the context of his interpersonal relations, and this new understanding was accompanied by the development of techniques for more adaptive, less conflictual, and more satisfying ways of relating to others. An integral part of this learning experience was undoubtedly the achievement of a sense of mastery over what had hitherto been seen as events to be endured passively. Conceptualizations of this process may be found in the writings of a host of therapists, from Freud to Erikson, but it has seldom been documented by the people who have experienced it.

The majority of the changes noted on the questionnaires could be subsumed under the general heading of "anxiety reduction." It should be recalled that the term "anxiety" has two distinct meanings in psychoanalytic literature. Phenomenally, the term refers to a particular affect, the well-known sensations of uneasiness, apprehension, dread, fear, or simply "vague anxiety." These descriptions were grouped in our coding scheme, but obviously they do not exhaust the connotations of the term.

In another sense, anxiety may be viewed as a failure of psychic integration (Fingarette 1963) resulting from the individual's inability to integrate his life experiences and his own emotional needs. The signs of such failure may be any or all of the following: (1) anxiety affect as defined in the preceding paragraph, (2) somatic anxiety "equivalents" (e.g., psychosomatic symptoms), and (3) defensive alignments and attitudes which prevent further personality disintegration.

In addition to these signs, adaptive failure frequently (but not always) evokes feelings of being overwhelmed and powerless in the face of some inner threat. As Fromm-Reichmann (1954) put it, "In going over the literature on anxiety in children and adults, from M. Klein, Sharpe and Spitz, to Ferenczi and Rank, Freud, Rado, and Sullivan, Fromm, Horney and Silverberg, it seems that the feelings of powerlessness, of helplessness in the presence of inner dangers, which the individual cannot control, constitutes in the last analysis the common background of all further elaborations on the theory of anxiety." Precisely these feelings permeated both the presenting complaints and the areas of improvement listed by our patients. Gradually, in the course of therapy, feelings of confidence, assurance, and mastery replaced helplessness, inadequacy, and overwhelming despair. In psychoanalytic terms, the patient's natural tendencies toward synthesis, meaning, organization, competence, and growth supplanted his sense of failure and helplessness.

The Durability of Therapeutic Change

Our study provided convincing evidence for the durability of therapeutic results. Two years or more after their last therapeutic contact a large proportion of our respondents found it unnecessary to seek further therapy, and there were few indications that this decision was the result of disillusionment. On the whole, they reported that they had developed a greater tolerance for frustration and a greater willingness to accept limitations in themselves, in others, and in their life situation, and described themselves as getting along relatively well. In view of the paucity of follow-up studies, these findings are even more significant than they might otherwise be.

A FORMULA FOR SUCCESS

A central question facing the researcher in psychotherapy is that of therapeutic effectiveness. It is clear that the kind of interpersonal relationship which Frank (1961) found in faith healing, thought control, and conversion, as well as in psychotherapy, is conducive to changes which may be described as therapeutic. However, the more basic investigation, from the point of view of psychotherapy as an empirical science, is to determine the specific changes produced by specific procedures in a specific group of patients. It is less important to prove that diverse forms of psychological intervention produce changes in certain individuals which can be described as "therapeutic" or to search for techniques applicable to all patients under all conditions than it is to isolate, describe, and test the operations which, under specified conditions, will produce given results in individuals with given problems. It is immaterial whether such results will obtain only in a narrow segment of the population, although it may turn out that this is indeed the case. What does matter a great deal is that the procedures be made explicit, that they be compared and tested against other possible alternatives, and that the results (within limits) be predictable. Even under these utopian conditions considerable uncertainty will remain simply because human beings cannot be isolated from the host of social, psychological, and maturational influences which impinge on them during their therapy as at other times in their lives. The contribution of this sort of research will come from its delineation and specification of therapeutic procedures, and any such study of necessity will examine the interaction between the personality of the therapist and that of the patient.

In this connection it is important to remember Freud's extreme caution in making claims for psychoanalysis as a therapeutic procedure (see his 1937 paper in Freud 1950). He saw its applications as rather narrowly circumscribed, and, if anything, he erred on the side of conservatism by excluding a host of disorders as unsuitable for psychoanalysis. The "overselling" of psychoanalysis must therefore be laid at the doorsteps of some of his more ambitious disciples.

9.

THE YIELD

At this point we take a broader look at the implications of our work for patients—both prospective and past—therapists, teachers of therapists, directors of outpatient clinics, and researchers. As far as the current practice and the future of individual psychotherapy is concerned, what we find is both heartening and disappointing. There can be no doubt that outpatient psychotherapy performs a highly useful function and that certain patients may be expected to derive substantial benefit from it. Such treatment, however, is not for everyone. Most of the patients represented in our studies were young, intelligent, well educated, and members of the middle class. Since psychotherapy is time-consuming, expensive, and emotionally and intellectually demanding, private outpatient treatment is restricted to the relatively affluent members of American society, and this state of affairs is likely to remain unchanged for some time to come. The fact that many experienced therapists see a few patients at reduced fees is a testimony to their sense of social responsibility, but the number of persons reached in this way is, to be realistic, insignificant.

As we have seen, a large segment of individuals who do not fit this description and who apply for service to out-patient clinics, mental health centers, and similar public agencies obtain relatively little help. This is in part a function of the discrepancy between the kinds of services offered by such agencies and the needs of their clients. It is true that in recent years the scope of mental health services has been broadened considerably and they have become more readily available, yet they remain pitifully inadequate.

Who Is Selected for Individual Psychotherapy?

Of the large number of emotionally troubled persons who turn for help to outpatient clinics, only a very small percentage has the good fortune to receive psychotherapy for any substantial period of time. A large proportion of applicants never get to see a therapist, and the relatively few who do frequently stay for only a few sessions. The problem involves selection on the part of the potential patient as well as of the clinic. Services are not offered to many people who seek help, but when they are, many people do not take advantage of them. The reasons for rejecting an offer of psychotherapy are difficult to assess: some people obviously are not serious about entering psychotherapy; some have erroneous notions about it and reject it when they become aware of the need for their active participation; some become discouraged by the reception accorded them by the agency to which they apply; some find the prospect of self-examination extremely threatening; coming regularly to a clinic entails too many sacrifices for others.

Many persons in our culture still have considerable inhibitions and reservations about consulting a psychotherapist, and the wish—both conscious and unconscious—to view unhappiness and emotional suffering as a physical ailment is widespread. There is no stigma attached to consulting a physician, and it is not surprising that people most readily turn for help to a general practitioner or internist. They find the pronouncement that they are suffering from a vitamin deficiency, an allergy, or even a heart condition easier to accept than that their difficulties are symptoms of disturbed interpersonal relations, such as excessive dependency on a spouse, seething hatred of a parent, and the like. The fear of being labeled "crazy," "a mental case," "homosexual," etc., is far from extinct despite the influence of books, magazines, motion pictures, and television. To be "in psychotherapy" or, preferably, "in psychoanalysis" is acceptable—even a sign of status and prestige—among many intellectuals in the larger urban centers but is virtually unknown elsewhere.

It is rare for a person to become aware that he is in need of psychotherapy and to come to a therapist on his own. In a university setting a common source of referrals is the student health service, whose staff members are alert to emotional problems even when presented in the guise of other complaints. In the community physicians with an eye for the emotional factors in illness are still not numerous, although their number is steadily increasing, and family doctors often attempt to help their patients through reassurance and understanding and refer them to a psychiatrist, psychologist, or mental health clinic only as a last resort.

In view of the massive attempts which are being made to educate the public about the nature of psychotherapeutic help, we may question whether the information which is being dispensed by the mass media is as useful as it might be. Since the beginning of the modern mental health movement, efforts have been made to remove the stigma of emotional problems by defining them as an "illness" (Szasz 1961). It is hardly surprising, then, that emotional problems have come to be seen in terms of a medical "disease model," an attitude encouraged by the use of such terms as "patient," "treatment," "cure," and so on. The psychotherapist, on the other hand, attempts to make his patients see neurosis as a problem of maladaptation, faulty learning, and the like. The patient comes to realize that he is not the victim of a disease visited upon him by mysterious forces and that he must take an active part in his own treatment. It follows that neurosis must be generally understood as a problem in living and adaptation.

We turn now from the patient who rejects psychotherapy to the individual willing to accept help who finds it unavailable. For a patient to be accepted for individual psychotherapy, he must meet the criterion of a "good" patient: he must impress the clinic (and his prospective therapist) as a good candidate for psychotherapy, in the sense that a therapist is willing to make a significant emotional commitment to him. It should be pointed out that this consideration is altogether valid. The psychotherapist, unlike other professionals, is called upon to make a very considerable emotional investment in the patients he accepts for therapy. Like other professionals he must have a sense of social responsibility, humanitarianism, and desire to help, but no other professional is expected to give so much of himself, to immerse himself so deeply in another person's intimate personal problems, and to weather such emotional storms as those to which many patients subject their therapists. To see a person for one or two hours a week over a period of a year is a major commitment which must not be underestimated. With all the good will in the world, the psychotherapist cannot be expected to make such a commitment unless he can convince himself that for professional as well as personal reasons the project is worth while.

Because most of the therapists in our study were in training, they were not motivated by financial factors: the patients paid little, and therapists received no direct financial return in any case. On the other hand, they may have been more likely to accept a patient who, while perhaps not a promising candidate for psychotherapy, presented an "interesting" clinical problem or some other challenge. Not all patients were selected by the therapist; at times patients were assigned by a senior staff member, although a therapist was rarely compelled to see a patient not of his choice for a prolonged period.

Low Prestige of Short-Term Psychotherapy

It is a paradox that in America brief, short-term psychotherapy in outpatient clinics is usually administered by relative novices, whereas psychoanalysis or intensive psychotherapy is conducted by more highly experienced therapists whose work is supervised much more closely. The exigencies of intensive therapy do demand scrupulous guidence by an expert, but brief psychotherapy has its pitfalls as well. Premature interpretations by an unskilled therapist can prove useless or even destructive. Several authoritative writers in the field have called attention to this anomaly, pointing out that brief or clinic-type psychotherapy, far from being easy, requires a very high level of skill, extensive knowledge of psychodynamics, and careful technical management.

Even among novices, of course, there are great variations in skill. In our sample the level of competence of most of the therapists appears to have been reasonably adequate, and patients were usually treated with understanding, tact, and respect. They were "special" in that they were seen by residents rather than medical students and had at least 25 hours of treatment. It has been pointed out that most patients seen in the clinic studied receive less than 25 hours of therapy, and many are seen by medical students under staff or resident supervision. In the six years preceding the study only 13 per cent of the clinic population had 20 or more hours of therapy. In asking the question of who should carry out psychotherapy, therefore, we wish to call attention to the possible effects of what we believe to be common practice in outpatient training facilities: we are not concerned with the particular patient population surveyed here.

In collecting our data it became apparent to us that the patient population used to train neophyte therapists (i.e., medical students and beginning psychology graduate students) is drawn from socioeconomically deprived groups. As the trainee acquires more experience, more and more of his patients come from the middle class. The practical reasons for this state of affairs have been discussed, but professionals are not thereby relieved from responsibility for the possible consequences of such practices.

Therapy can do harm. When we permit a completely inexperienced person to "do psychotherapy," we are saying, by implication, that such treatment is, in essence, harmless. Would we apply the same rationale to a surgical procedure? The amount of damage done by a beginning psychotherapist may be small and, if his patients are carefully selected, may be kept to a minimum. Furthermore, many young therapists have a good measure of native talent, which may compensate in part for their lack of experience, but talent is no substitute for technical expertise. To be sure, students in any field must begin somewhere, but stringent safeguards must be observed. The thorny problem of the training of psychotherapists is beyond the scope of this discussion, but we feel compelled to point out that the view that a "little bit of psychotherapy is good for everybody" is highly irresponsible. The question of precisely what constitutes an adequate level of therapeutic competence has not been answered, nor are therapists and researchers as clear about acceptable practices as is desirable.

IMPORTANCE OF THE INTERPERSONAL EXPERIENCE

Perhaps the most significant finding in our investigation was the constellation of data pointing toward the importance of interpersonal relationships in emotional problems. Difficulty with significant figures in one's current life situation was among the most frequently mentioned presenting problems; improvement in interpersonal relationships was frequently given as the most important change resulting from therapy; and difficulties in such relationships were mentioned most frequently as a persisting problem. The treatment situation itself is, of course, an interpersonal one, and this fact is undoubtedly most significant. People develop neurotic problems in the context of interpersonal relationships, and the new relationship with a therapist provides an opportunity for resolving them (Sullivan 1953; Fromm-Reichmann 1950).

Many patients also pointed to an improved self-image as a major success of their therapy. It is likely that this kind of change is the result of an increase in interpersonal skills. When a person is absorbed in his inner problems, conflicts, and needs, he has little energy available for relationships with other people. This being the case, he is interested in others only to the extent that they satisfy his dependency or flatter his weakened ego, not in their needs or wants. This "selfishness"—"self-centeredness" may be more precise—is often perceived by the significant other.

Because he is always giving without ever having a chance to receive, the other resents being exploited and withdraws his support and interest. The patient is thus not only frustrated by not having his emotional needs met but, more important, is deprived of the rewards, satisfactions, and sense of achievement which helping and supporting others would give him. The experience of learning to give as well as receive, with increments in self-esteem as a result, may be one of the most important products of therapy. Increased receptivity to interpersonal experience may, of course, be the result of a better understanding of one's neurotic patterns.

It is well known that one of the concomitants of emotional difficulty is a sense of estrangement. Patients frequently complain of having no one to talk to and of being unable to discuss their problems with members of their family. Therapy helps to reverse this trend. Patients often report greater ability to express their feelings toward spouses and family members and greater readiness to risk the pain of a more open and honest sharing of feelings.

The relationship with the therapist provides a model for dealing with other people. However, translations from therapy to everyday life are more easily achieved if there is a close relationship outside of therapy which is similarly intimate and consistent. New role models can be tested on a significant other person, such as a spouse. Such a relationship offers the patient the opportunity for "instant feedback" from someone who "counts" and who, unlike the therapist, is not restrained from making a direct emotional response. Such reality testing can be swift and dramatic, both positively and negatively. Therapy may give the patient the courage to initiate change, but in the final analysis it is the reaction of other people to his groping efforts which provide the real proving ground for the learning acquired in therapy (Goldstein, Heller and Sechrest 1966).

In support of this view, it should be noted that there were more than twice as many single people in the failure group, although the total sample was equally divided in marital status. Most single members of the failure group were young college students who were, at the same time, in the process of achieving autonomy as adults. Students are in a transition period of changing allegiances and are temporarily alone. For this reason, relationships with girl friends assume increased significance for the late adolescent, but a girl friend is not a wife.

Helping the patient to form a significant interpersonal relationship is certainly an important goal of psychotherapy; neurotic problems often prevent a person from reaching this objective alone. Because group relationships provide interactions which most closely parallel the student's life situation, and because close, intimate relationships are subordinated to peer group interactions during adolescence, it is possible that group psychotherapy would hold greater promise for most such patients than intense, prolonged, individual psychotherapy. This notion should be thoroughly explored.

Type and Quality of Therapy

Because of lack of comprehensive data on such patient-therapist interaction and gaps in our knowledge about the nature of therapy in general, we do not as yet know how personality and behavior changes are achieved. Our survey did provide some useful clues, however. Our therapists did not attempt radical personality change. They helped their patients work through certain traumatic experiences, clarified some patterns of neurotic interaction, and, above all, provided a corrective emotional experience (Alexander and French 1946).

Perhaps the most important aspect of these therapeutic encounters was this patient-therapist interaction. Patients experienced a hitherto unknown degree of acceptance, understanding, and respect, and within a framework of benevolent neutrality and warmth they were encouraged to examine some of the more troublesome aspects of their behavior and attitudes. This experience provided a sharp contrast to other human relationships they had known. It could be set up against the criticism, exploitation, and dependency which they had either encouraged themselves or of which they had been victims; it permitted expression of shameful, anxiety-provoking, and painful feelings; and it supplied them with a professional helper who insisted that they examine some of the problems in their lives and work out—on an emotional as well as a cognitive level—viable solutions.

No matter how faltering and imperfect the therapists' procedures, there is little question that self-acceptance, self-respect, and competence increased as a result. Broad psychoanalytic principles were generally employed, rather than persuasion, suggestion, and the like. There is reason to believe that these procedures, at least in principle, are teachable, communicable, and replicable. Perhaps more could have been done within the available time by experts using more sophisticated techniques, but something tangible was achieved.

The skeptic who insists on seeing the presenting symptom as the problem and denies the importance of intrapsychic conflicts and underlying causes will not be convinced by these demonstrations. He will counter that the patients' reports merely reflect the therapists' persuasiveness or their success in instilling faith in the authority of the healer. We do not know what the patients' retrospective accounts would have been had they been treated by therapists of a different theoretical orientation, but for a very large proportion the therapist appears to have succeeded in becoming a "good parent figure," and this image was essentially intact well beyond the termination of therapy. Although most of our patients were reasonably mature, as shown by their ability to function despite their neurotic handicaps, it is equally important to note that many of them were suffering from chronic and severe difficulties in living and yet were helped markedly by psychotherapy of the outpatient clinic variety.

Concluding Comments

Our investigation has yielded impressive evidence for individual psychotherapy on an outpatient basis, provided that patients are carefully selected and other circumstances are propitious. These results are strikingly similar to the conclusions which Berenson and Carkhuff have drawn from a careful review of the research on counseling and psychotherapy. Their findings may be paraphrased as follows:*

1. There is substantial evidence that therapists of very different orientations can be equally effective.

2. There is substantial evidence that therapeutic changes occur in a broad front and that they are independent of the therapist's theoretical position and professional affiliation.

3. There is substantial evidence that the efficacy of psychotherapy is primarily a function of a central core of facilitative conditions. These are three: (a) experiential, (b) didactic, and (c) the role model which the therapist provides. This formulation allows for the possibility that

* This summary is adapted and condensed from material presented on pp. 439–49 of *Sources of gain in counseling and psychotherapy*, ed. Bernard G. Berenson and Robert R. Carkhuff. Copyright © 1967 by Holt, Rinehart and Winston, Inc. Used by permission of Holt, Rinehart and Winston, Inc.

within the context of the core facilitative conditions a variety of techniques may enhance therapeutic effectiveness. These techniques, however, remain to be spelled out.

4. There is substantial evidence that facilitative conditions are not entities in themselves, to be communicated by prescribed techniques, but rather that they are present in all effective human encounters.

5. There is substantial evidence that techniques are rehabilitative when they free the individual to engage more fully in the kinds of life activities in which he would have become involved if the facilitative conditions had been present originally.

6. There is substantial evidence that all interpersonal encounters may have constructive or deteriorative consequences. To the extent that psychotherapy is effective, it maximizes the constructive consequences of the patient-therapist encounter.

7. There is substantial evidence that effective psychotherapy provides the patient with a human experience which is the inverse of the experiences which gave rise to the difficulties in the first place.

8. There is substantial evidence that in effective psychotherapy the patient eventually incorporates into his own life style the facilitative conditions offered him in therapy. He is influenced by the significant sources of learning in therapy to become more open, understanding, and respectful of himself and others. Thus, what he is learning is new techniques of effective living.

We fully subscribe to Berenson and Carkhuff's plea for the development of "preferred modes of treatment." As we have pointed out, researchers must examine the problem of *amenability to given forms of treatment*, including such departures from "traditional" psychotherapy as behavior therapy and operant conditioning. The utility of various outcome measures, such as reports by patients themselves and by persons close to them, assessments by experts, and objective data (e.g., job effectiveness, productivity, and the like) should be evaluated. Our research has strengthened our conviction, which we consider insufficiently appreciated by behavioristic psychologists, that in effective psychotherapy the patient makes gains which are subjective and defy quantification. Such gains include interpersonal competence, mastery, and increased self-esteem.

Effectiveness has become the goal of any therapeutic approach and the measure of its popularity and value. This point of view was forcefully put forward by Eysenck (1952), who alleged that psychotherapists in general had failed to demonstrate the efficacy of their procedures. While his initial argument, buttressed by data which were open to interpretations other than his, emphasized the absence of strong evidence in favor of psychotherapy, he and a host of followers have more recently asserted the superiority of behaviorally oriented methods and have presented a considerable body of empirical data to substantiate their claims.

The typical clinician is convinced of the worth of his therapeutic endeavors and, like Freud, is unimpressed by "statistics." As we have seen, a large majority of patients feel benefited by their psychotherapeutic experience. To an important degree, the question revolves around one's definition of "improvement." As one of the present authors has attempted to show (Strupp 1963), the kinds of improvement psychoanalysts are talking about appear to be vastly different from the criteria Eysenck (1952, 1961) invokes, but in either case the criteria must be *specifiable*. If a behavior therapist is willing to consider the alleviation of a snake phobia in an otherwise well-functioning personality a "cure," that is his privilege, and he cannot be challenged by other therapists, nor can he challenge those who work toward different objectives. But it is incumbent upon all therapists to be explicit about their goals. Knight's (1941) criteria, for example (disappearance of presenting symptoms, real improvement in mental functioning, and improved reality adjustment), may be too vague to serve as guidelines here, but they are specifiable in principle.

The scientific community and the public have a right to know the rules by which the therapeutic game is played, and they are entitled to accept or reject them. Analytic therapists, it seems to us, have devoted insufficient attention to this problem and in general have shrugged off the research's insistence upon evidence as indicative of ignorance or ulterior motives. If it is true, as Szasz (1967) asserts, that learning in psychoanalysis is entirely different from learning in behavior therapy—if the former is principally concerned with increasing the patient's sphere of autonomy rather than alleviating his symptoms—there must exist *some* measure of such increased autonomy. The evidence must be communicable and at least in some way must be tied to the patient's behavior.

The chaos pervading the entire area of psychotherapy and psychotherapeutic research, to which several authors (Colby 1964; Matarazzo 1965) have called attention, is at least partly attributable to the failure to specify the precise nature of the operations which are designed to achieve a given objective in a given patient. We cannot ignore the simple fact that a patient comes to a psychotherapist because of a "problem" for which he is seeking a solution. No matter how the problem is conceptualized or attacked, the end result must be a change demonstrable by the scientific rules of evidence.

The therapist is entirely within his rights in specifying his goals and the criteria of success that he is willing to accept. Other members of the community may consider these goals unimportant, incommensurate with the effort expended, impractical, or trivial, and these are value judgments, as are all outcome criteria in the final analysis. But once the therapist has stated his goals and his techniques, his work must be judged accordingly. We are convinced that if therapists as a group made concerted efforts along these lines, the record of psychoanalytic therapy would be vastly more impressive than is suggested by the existing literature.

To elaborate on the choice of criteria, in this country today we find a strong emphasis on behavioral criteria, epitomized by the question, does the patient act differently after psychotherapy? He may interact differently with his spouse, his children, his boss; he may become more assertive with people in general, engage in activities he previously avoided, and so on. Any form of psychotherapy worthy of the name must be capable of producing such changes (or inducing the patient to make them). But, as is shown in our survey, there is also a wide range of internal changes which are notoriously difficult to specify, observe, and measure. In principle, internal changes are as real as behavioral ones, although one's personal preference may be for one rather than the other, and investigators committed to a behavoristic orientation may not consider them important. Until therapists committed to such changes become more articulate about their goals and subject them to systematic study, their assertions that their patients have become more mature, self-reliant, independent, and skillful in handling interpersonal situations will be ignored. It will be necessary to place greater weight on the patient's own testimony, as we have attempted to do here, and to build a bridge between subjective (necessarily fallible) and objective data.

The outstanding characteristic of neurosis, regardless of whether it is viewed as an "illness" or as a "problem in living," is pain: intense suffering, misery, anxiety, hopelessness, and despair. Novelists, poets, and philosophers have described these feelings, which defy quantification but which are undeniably real to anyone who has experienced them or has the capacity to empathize with them. Like any pain, neurotic suffering is a subjective state which cannot be captured by behavioral measures of any level of sophistication. To assess it in any meaningful way, we must rely on the patient's testimony. But how can one compare a person's feelings today with those of last year? How can one compare one person's pain with another's? Feelings fluctuate, they are elusive, people are suggestible, and their testimony may be highly unreliable.

In the face of these dilemmas, the behaviorist throws up his hands and turns to "behavioral indicators" which are observable by others and about which agreement can be reached. But do we have a right to ignore central aspects of life simply because we have found no effective ways of measuring them? To reiterate, it appears to us that the chaotic state of statistics on psychotherapeutic result is at least partially attributable to the researcher's inability or unwillingness to recognize this problem or indifference to it. It is symptomatic of this attitude that the issue is seldom discussed.

To be sure, changes in behavior often accompany changes in feeling states, but the relationship is not one-to-one, nor can behavioral change substitute for attitudinal change. Each therapist and patient can give abundant examples of behaviors which remain unchanged throughout therapy, while a given situation may be perceived and reacted to differently as a result of it. What value are we to place on such perceptions and reactions? If some form of psychotherapy never or only rarely produced changes in the patient's overt behavior, there would be considerable ground for skepticism about its utility, but it seems inordinately severe to restrict evaluations of psychotherapy to changes in overt behavior. The therapist is not obligated to play the game by any rules the critics impose; on the other hand, he has no mandate to label as "therapeutic" any procedure or activity he wishes. The burden of proof is upon the therapist, not upon the critic.

The conclusion we draw from all this is that the term psychotherapy as used today is a multifaceted conglomerate with fuzzy meanings; that as long as there is no reasonable consensus about methods, objectives, and outcomes, comparisons between different forms of therapy will remain largely meaningless; and that the effectiveness of psychotherapy is largely a problem of definition—of the investigator's (or the public's) value judgments about worthwhile outcomes. Because psychotherapy has traditionally been regarded as a kind of medical treatment, the concept of cure has often been employed as a seemingly reasonable criterion. We have shown the inappropriateness of this notion. Patients change, but no one is "cured" in the sense of being restored to a *status quo ante*, nor does there seem to be such a thing as "spontaneous remission"—certainly not among the patients we studied. It is safe to predict that when the changes that may be expected from particular psychotherapeutic procedures are specified, medical analogizing will be abandoned.

It would help greatly to view psychotherapy as a form of education or as Freud called it, "after-education." What the patient in psychotherapy acquires are new perceptions of himself and others; he learns new patterns of interpersonal behavior and unlearns maladaptive ones. There are vast individual differences in the capacity to profit from different kinds of learning situations. Psychoanalysis, as one form of psychotherapy, may be likened to graduate education, and, like graduate education, it is suitable only for relatively few people. To be sure, some deserving students are excluded from graduate school for financial reasons, but society is aware of the problem and attempts to remedy it through scholarships and the like. The same considerations should apply to prospective candidates for psychoanalysis or psychotherapy. The patient's suitability for a given form of therapy must be decided on factual or clinical grounds, rather than on the basis of his ability or inability to pay for an expensive service. For some persons, a form of "behavior modification" may be the best that can be hoped for; for others, the achievement of greater autonomy through self-discovery in psychoanalysis may be the goal. Within each category there will be slow and fast "learners." In each instance, the method must be tailored to the individual, which is why psychotherapeutic principles provide only the most general guidelines.

The psychotherapeutic situation is a unique vehicle for personal growth and maturation. It has much in common with other interpersonal experiences—openness, acceptance, and understanding. Similarity, however, is not identity. Qualities which set the psychotherapeutic situation apart from other human encounters are the therapist's objectivity; his sharply circumscribed involvement in the patient's life; his training, which enables him to detect neurotic entanglements and self-defeating maneuvers; and his commitment to help the patient arrive at his own solutions by the process of examining and understanding factors within himself which contribute to his difficulties.

At its best, individual psychotherapy creates a learning situation unequaled by anything else that human ingenuity has been able to devise. While costly in terms of money, time, manpower, and dedication of the participants to the common task, it remains one of the few monuments to the individual's worth, self-direction and independence in a collectivist society which fosters conformity and erodes individual values and autonomy in a host of ways. From a practical standpoint, it cannot begin to cope effectively with all human suffering caused by destructive interpersonal experiences, nor can any amount of refinement in technique increase its effectiveness to the point where it can be considered a universal weapon against neurotic problems. In essence, it is an unrealizable ideal of self-discovery through learning and teaching in the context of a human relationship uninfluenced by ulterior motives of any kind. What the patient, if he is fortunate, may receive is a glimpse, or perhaps even a reasonable approximation, of this ideal.

APPENDIXES

Appendix A

Questionnaire P: Patient's Form

Psychotherapy Questionnaire

This survey is part of a research project to study how former patients feel about their psychotherapy experience. Please try to answer all questions as completely and truthfully as you can. We ask you not to sign your name.

Please return the completed questionnaire in the envelope provided. Your cooperation in this research is very much appreciated. If you are interested in the results of this survey, you may send your request to the address below.

Psychotherapy Research Project
Department of Psychiatry
University of North Carolina
Chapel Hill, North Carolina

This research is supported by a research grant (MH02171) from the National Institute of Mental Health, Public Health Service.

OMIT NAME

1. Age*:
2. Sex (circle one):   M   F
3. Marital status*:   Single   Married   Divorced   Widowed
4. Number of children*:
5. Education* (check highest level and complete question):
   _____ Elementary school (indicate number of years:)
   _____ High school (indicate number of years:)
   _____ High school graduate
   _____ College (indicate number of years:)
   _____ College graduate
   _____ Graduate study or professional training (kind,
            degree, etc.):

   _____
   _____

6. Occupation*:
7. Annual family income (gross)*:
   _____ less than $5,000
   _____ between $5,000 and $7,500
   _____ between $7,500 and $10,000
   _____ between $10,000 and $12,500
   _____ between $12,500 and $15,000
   _____ between $15,000 and $20,000
   _____ more than $20,000
8.–12. Please give the information about your psychotherapy
       experience called for in the table. If you had more than
       one period of therapy or if you had more than one
       therapist, indicate to which period (or therapist) your
       answers to this questionnaire refer. Call your first thera-
       pist A, the second, if any, B, etc. If you returned to any
       therapist, such as Therapist A, after a period of time,
       repeat A and complete the question.

* At this time.

THE ANSWERS IN THIS QUESTIONNAIRE
REFER TO THERAPIST _____. (please indicate)

Therapist	A		
Beginning date Mo. Yr.			
Your age at the time			
Termination date Mo. Yr.			
Total number of hours			
Typical frequency of sessions per week			
Typical fee per hour			

15.* (a) If you had only one period of therapy, did you ever feel a need for further therapy? (check one)

_____ Never

_____ Very rarely

_____ A number of times

_____ Often

_____ Very often

(b) If you felt a need for further therapy, but did not seek it, what were your reasons?

16. How much in need of further therapy do you feel now?

_____ No need at all

_____ Slight need

_____ Could use more

* Occasionally you will find that item numbers are omitted.

_____ Considerable need
_____ Very great need

17. What led to the termination of your therapy?
_____ My decision
_____ My therapist's decision
_____ Mutual agreement
_____ External factors (describe briefly)

_____ Other (describe briefly)

18. How much have you benefited from your therapy?
_____ A great deal
_____ A fair amount
_____ To some extent
_____ Very little
_____ Not at all

19. Everything considered, how satisfied are you with the results of your psychotherapy experience?
_____ Extremely dissatisfied
_____ Moderately dissatisfied
_____ Fairly dissatisfied
_____ Fairly satisfied
_____ Moderately satisfied
_____ Highly satisfied
_____ Extremely satisfied

20. What are the reasons for your response?

21. Was your therapist of the same sex? _____ Yes _____ No

24. What impression did you have of his level of experience as a therapist?
_____ Extremely inexperienced
_____ Rather inexperienced
_____ Somewhat experienced
_____ Fairly experienced
_____ Highly experienced
_____ Exceptionally experienced

Please indicate to what extent each of the following statements describes your therapy experience. Disregard that at one point or another in therapy you may have felt differently. Use the following code and circle your answer.

+2 Strongly agree
+1 Mildly agree
 0 Undecided
−1 Mildly disagree
−2 Strongly disagree

+2 +1 0 −1 −2 25. My therapy was an intensely emotional experience.
+2 +1 0 −1 −2 26. My therapy was often a rather painful experience.
+2 +1 0 −1 −2 27. I remember very little about the details of my psychotherapeutic work.
+2 +1 0 −1 −2 28. My therapist almost never used technical terms.
+2 +1 0 −1 −2 29. On the whole I experienced very little feeling in the course of therapy.
+2 +1 0 −1 −2 30. There were times when I experienced intense anger toward my therapist.
+2 +1 0 −1 −2 31. I feel the therapist was rather active most of the time.
+2 +1 0 −1 −2 32. I am convinced that the therapist respected me as a person.
+2 +1 0 −1 −2 33. I feel the therapist was genuinely interested in helping me.
+2 +1 0 −1 −2 34. I often felt I was "just another patient."
+2 +1 0 −1 −2 35. The therapist was always keenly attentive to what I had to say.
+2 +1 0 −1 −2 36. The therapist often used very abstract language.
+2 +1 0 −1 −2 37. He very rarely engaged in small talk.
+2 +1 0 −1 −2 38. The therapist tended to be rather stiff and formal.
+2 +1 0 −1 −2 39. The therapist's manner was quite natural and unstudied.

+2 +1 0 −1 −2   40. I feel that he often didn't understand my feelings.

+2 +1 0 −1 −2   41. I feel he was extremely passive.

+2 +1 0 −1 −2   42. His general attitude was rather cold and distant.

+2 +1 0 −1 −2   43. I often had the feeling that he talked too much.

+2 +1 0 −1 −2   44. Nothing the therapist said or did ever decreased my self-respect.

+2 +1 0 −1 −2   45. I would not want to be without my psychotherapy experience for anything in the world.

+2 +1 0 −1 −2   46. I was never sure whether the therapist thought I was a worthwhile person.

+2 +1 0 −1 −2   47. I had a feeling of absolute trust in the therapist's integrity as a person.

+2 +1 0 −1 −2   48. I felt there usually was a good deal of warmth in the way he talked to me.

+2 +1 0 −1 −2   49. The tone of his statements tended to be rather cold.

+2 +1 0 −1 −2   50. The tone of his statements tended to be rather neutral.

+2 +1 0 −1 −2   51. I was never given any instructions or advice on how to conduct my life.

+2 +1 0 −1 −2   52. The therapist often talked about psychoanalytic theory in my sessions.

+2 +1 0 −1 −2   53. A major emphasis in treatment was upon my attitudes and feelings about the therapist.

+2 +1 0 −1 −2   54. A major emphasis in treatment was upon my relationships with people in my current life.

+2 +1 0 −1 −2   55. A major emphasis in treatment was upon childhood experiences.

+2 +1 0 −1 −2   56. A major emphasis in treatment was upon gestures, silences, shifts in my tone of voice, and bodily movements.

+2 +1 0 −1 −2   57. I was almost never given any reassurances by the therapist.

+2 +1 0 −1 −2   58. I had the feeling that the therapist sometimes criticized things I did or said.

+2 +1 0 −1 −2   59. My therapist showed very little interest in my dreams and fantasies.

+2 +1 0 −1 −2   60. I usually felt I was fully accepted by the therapist.

+2 +1 0 −1 −2   61. I never had the slightest doubt about the therapist's interest in helping me.

+2 +1 0 −1 −2   62. I was often uncertain about the therapist's real feelings toward me.

+2 +1 0 −1 −2   63. The therapist's manner of speaking seemed rather formal.

+2 +1 0 −1 −2   64. I feel the *emotional* experience of therapy was much more important in producing change than *intellectual* understanding of my problems.

+2 +1 0 −1 −2   65. My therapist stressed intellectual understanding as much as emotional experiencing.

66. What were your major complaints (symptoms) that led you to enter therapy, i.e., how did you view your problem(s) at the beginning of therapy?

67. How well did you feel you were getting along then?
_____ Very well
_____ Fairly well
_____ Neither well nor poorly
_____ Fairly poorly
_____ Very poorly
_____ Extremely poorly

68. How long before entering therapy did you feel in need of professional help?
_____ less than 1 year
_____ 1–2 years
_____ 3–4 years
_____ 5–10 years
_____ 11–15 years
_____ 16–20 years
_____ years
(specify)

69. How severely disturbed did you consider yourself at the beginning of your therapy?

Extremely disturbed	Very much disturbed	Moderately disturbed	Somewhat disturbed	Very slightly disturbed

70. How much anxiety did you feel at the time you started therapy?

A tremendous amount	A great deal	A fair amount	Very little	None at all

71. How great was the internal "pressure" to do something about these problems when you entered psychotherapy?
_____ Extremely great
_____ Very great
_____ Fairly great
_____ Relatively small
_____ Very small
_____ Extremely small

73. How much do you feel you have changed as a result of psychotherapy?
_____ A great deal
_____ A fair amount
_____ Somewhat
_____ Very little
_____ Not at all

74. Describe the most important changes you have experienced.

75. How much of this change do you feel has been apparent to others?

(a) People closest to you (husband, wife, etc.)

A great deal	A fair amount	Somewhat	Very little	Not at all

(b) Close friends

A great deal	A fair amount	Somewhat	Very little	Not at all

(c) Co-workers, acquaintances, etc.

A great deal	A fair amount	Somewhat	Very little	Not at all

76. On the whole how well do you feel you are getting along now?

_____ Extremely well
_____ Very well
_____ Fairly well
_____ Neither well nor poorly
_____ Fairly poorly
_____ Very poorly
_____ Extremely poorly

77. What kinds of problems, if any, do you feel exist now
(unresolved and/or new ones)?

78. How adequately do you feel you are dealing with any
present problems?
_____ Very adequately
_____ Fairly adequately
_____ Neither adequately nor inadequately
_____ Somewhat inadequately
_____ Very inadequately
79. To what extent have your complaints or symptoms that
brought you to therapy changed as a result of treatment?
_____ Completely disappeared
_____ Very greatly improved
_____ Considerably improved
_____ Somewhat improved
_____ Not at all improved
_____ Got worse

80. How soon after entering therapy did you feel any marked change?

_____ months and/or _____ hours of therapy (approximately)

81. In general, how would you describe your attitude toward the therapist?

84. What adjectives do you feel best describe the therapist's attitude toward you while you were in therapy?

88. How strongly would you recommend psychotherapy to a close friend with emotional problems?
   _____ Would strongly recommend it
   _____ Would mildly recommend it
   _____ Would recommend it but with some reservations
   _____ Would not recommend it
   _____ Would advise against it
89. Please indicate the adequacy of this questionnaire in describing your therapy experience. Give any additional data which you feel are relevant to an understanding of your experience.

Appendix B

Questionnaire T: Therapist's Form

Psychotherapy Questionnaire (Therapist's Form)

Patient's name or identification: _____

Period of therapy _____

Dear Doctor:

Some time ago you were kind enough to send a follow-up questionnaire to some of your former psychotherapy patients. In order to help us analyze the results of this survey we would appreciate your giving us some information about these patients even though some of them failed to return a questionnaire. Incidentally, the responses of your patients are available to you at any time (preferably after you have filled out this questionnaire). Thank you very much for your cooperation.

Please rate each of the following items, comparing the patient with other patients whom you see in psychotherapy.

		Very little	Some	Moderate	Fairly great	Very great
1. Defensiveness	before	____	____	____	____	____
	after	____	____	____	____	____
2. Anxiety	before	____	____	____	____	____
	after	____	____	____	____	____
3. Ego strength	before	____	____	____	____	____
	after	____	____	____	____	____
4. Degree of disturbance	before	____	____	____	____	____
	after	____	____	____	____	____
5. Capacity for insight	before	____	____	____	____	____
	after	____	____	____	____	____
6. Over-all adjustment	before	____	____	____	____	____
	after	____	____	____	____	____
7. Personal liking for patient	before	____	____	____	____	____
	after	____	____	____	____	____
8. Motivation for therapy	before	____	____	____	____	____
9. Improvement expected (prognosis)	before	____	____	____	____	____
10. Degree to which countertransference was a problem in therapy		____	____	____	____	____

163

	Very little	Some	Mod-erate	Fairly great	Very great
11. Degree to which you usually enjoy working with this kind of patient in psychotherapy	—	—	—	—	—
12. Degree of symptomatic improvement	—	—	—	—	—
13. Degree of change in basic personality structure	—	—	—	—	—
14. Degree to which you felt warmly toward the patient	—	—	—	—	—
15. How much of an "emotional investment" did you have in this patient?	—	—	—	—	—
16. Degree to which you think the patient felt warmly toward you	—	—	—	—	—
17. Over-all success of therapy	—	—	—	—	—

18. How would you characterize your working relationship with this patient?

Extremely poor	Fairly poor	Neither good nor poor	Fairly good	Extremely good

19. How satisfied do you think the patient was with the results of his therapy?

Extremely dissatisfied	Fairly dissatisfied	Neither satisfied nor dissatisfied	Fairly satisfied	Extremely satisfied

20. How would you characterize the form of psychotherapy you conducted with this patient?

```
|_____|_____|_____|_____|
```
Largely   Intensive
supportive   analytical

21. Do you recall any strikingly pleasant experiences that you had during the therapy sessions with this patient? Yes _____ No _____ If yes, please circle the number that best indicates the degree of pleasantness.

    1   2   3   4   5   6   7   8   9
Mildly pleasant   Extremely pleasant

22. Do you recall any strikingly unpleasant experiences you had with this patient? Yes_____No_____. If yes, please circle the number that best indicates the degree of unpleasantness.

    1   2   3   4   5   6   7   8   9
Mildly unpleasant   Extremely unpleasant

23. Over-all, how would you characterize your experiences with this patient?

    1   2   3   4   5   6   7   8   9
Unpleasant   Pleasant

Additional comments (please use reverse side, if necessary):

Appendix C
Clinic Chart Data Sheet

1. Patient's name: _____

Last   First   Middle

2. Clinic file no.: _____
3. Age*:
4. Sex: M   F
5. Marital status*:   Single   Married   Separated or Divorced   Widowed
6. Number of children*:
7. Education* (check highest level and complete question):
   _____ Elementary school (indicate number of years:)
   _____ High school (indicate number of years:)
   _____ High school graduate
   _____ College (indicate number of years:)
   _____ College graduate
   _____ Graduate study or professional training (kind, degree, etc.):

   _____

   _____

8. Occupation* (in case of married women, give husband's occupation):
   1   Higher executives, proprietors of large concerns, and major professionals
   2   Business managers, proprietors of medium-sized concerns, and lesser professionals
   3   Administrative personnel, small independent businessmen, and minor professionals
   4   Clerical and sales workers, technicians, and owners of small businesses
   5   Skilled manual employees
   6   Machine operators and semi-skilled employees
   7   Unskilled employees
   x   Students
   y   Housewives
   z   Other (unemployed, unknown)
9. Annual family income (gross)*:
   _____ less than $3,000
   _____ between $3,000 and $3,999
   _____ between $4,000 and $4,999

* At time of first interview.

169

_____ between $5,000 and $7,499
_____ between $7,500 and $9,999
_____ between $10,000 and $12,499
_____ between $12,500 and $14,999
_____ $15,000 or more

10. Therapist's name | Beginning date Mo. Year | Termina-tion date Mo. Year | Total hours | Typical frequency of sessions | Typical fee per hour

_____

_____

_____

11. Therapist's sex in relation to patient's: Same _____ Opposite _____
12. Therapist's professional affiliation*:
    _____ Resident in psychiatry
    _____ Psychology student or intern
    _____ Psychiatrist (staff)
    _____ Psychologist (staff)
    _____ Social worker (staff)
13. Hospitalizations*:
    _____ Yes   Number of times, dates, length, location:
                       _____
                       _____
    _____ No
    _____ Unknown
14. Prominent presenting symptoms*:

15. How long before entering therapy did patient seem to have troublesome symptoms?
    _____ less than 1 year
    _____ 1–2 years
    _____ 3–4 years
    _____ 5–10 years
    _____ more than 10 years

	Very little	Some	Mod-erate	Fairly great	Very great
16. Amount of subjective discomfort*	___	___	___	___	___
17. Degree of impairment*	___	___	___	___	___
18. Patient's motivation for therapy*	___	___	___	___	___
19. Degree of improvement expected (prognosis)*	___	___	___	___	___
20. Degree of symptomatic improvement	___	___	___	___	___
21. Over-all success of therapy	___	___	___	___	___

22. Prominent changes in patient as a result of therapy:

23. What led to the termination of therapy?
　　___ Patient's decision
　　___ Therapist's decision
　　___ Mutual agreement
　　___ External factors (describe briefly)

24. Final diagnosis:

[25. Not used.]
26. Birthplace: _____
　　　　　　　　　　City　　　　　　State
27. Residence*: _____
　　　　　　　　　　City　　　　　　State
28. ___ Rural ___ Urban
29. Distance traveled to NCMH (miles)*:
30. Religious preference:
31. Referred by:
　　___ Family physician

_____ Psychiatrist (not NCMH)
_____ NCMH medical service
_____ Student health
_____ Other hospital
_____ Minister
_____ Social service agency
_____ Self
_____ Other (specify):

32. Date of initial contact at OPD:
33. Date of first OPD therapy interview:
34. Disposition between first contact and therapy:
_____ Waiting list
_____ Hospitalized
_____ Unable to contact or no reply
_____ Other (specify):

35. Time elapsed between first contact and OPD therapy (weeks):
36. Therapy previous to NCMH contact: ____ Yes ____ No
37. Length of previous therapy (hours):
38. Drug therapy: ____ Yes ____ No
39. Type of drug:
Dosage (if available):
Dates of administration (if available):
40. Canceled interviews:
_____ Very frequent
_____ Frequent
_____ Occasional
_____ Rare
_____ None
41. Reason for termination:
_____ Therapist left NCMH or service
_____ Patient moved away
_____ Patient stopped coming
_____ Mutual agreement that goal had been reached; no further need for therapy (exclusive of patient's or therapist's moving)
_____ Other (specify):

Appendix D

The Problem of Sample Bias

In order to determine the extent to which patients who returned completed questionnaires might represent a biased sample, the original sample was subdivided into the three groups shown in Table D-1. Objective data from the clinic charts on these groups were then compared.

Table D-1. Frequency Distributions and Chi Square Tests for Respondents vs. Non-Respondents

Rating	Groups 1 and 2[a]	Group 3[b]	Total	χ^2	p
6. Degree of Impairment					
Very little, Some (1, 2)	5	17	22		
Moderate (3)	28	62	90		
Fairly great (4)	31	36	67	8.22	.05
Very great (5)	9	7	16		
8. Degree of Improvement Expected					
Some (2)	32	22	54		
Moderate (3)	30	76	106	15.72	.01
Fairly great (4)	10	24	34		
20. Number of Prior Hospitalizations					
None	25	59	84		
1 or more	38	46	84	4.29	.05
28. Referral Source					
Family physician (1)	9	29	38		
Psychiatrist, not NCMH (2)	13	9	22		
Medical hospitals (3, 4, 5)	17	37	54		
Minister, social service (6, 7)	4	12	16	12.55	.05
Self (8)	6	10	16		
NCMH inpatient (9)	24	24	48		

[a] Group 1: questionnaire returned; patient refused to complete. Group 2: no reply.
[b] Completed questionnaire returned by patient.
NOTE: Non-significant items were omitted.

Only four items yielded statistically significant results: non-respondents tended to be rated higher in degree of impairment, tended to have a poorer prognosis, exceeded respondents in previous hospitalizations and were more likely to have been referred by a psychiatrist and to have been inpatients at the North Carolina Memorial Hospital.

The conclusion emerges that patients whose therapy was successful were more likely to respond to the questionnaire, with the result that they are probably somewhat over-represented in the survey.

Appendix E

Rater Agreement on Global
Clinical Judgments

The task of rating the total sample of 244 patients was divided between two research assistants, hereafter referred to as RA 1 and RA 2, who were fully familiar with the project and its objectives. To ensure that the two assessments would be comparable, scale points for each item were defined as follows:

16. Amount of subjective discomfort
    Subjective discomfort is the phenomenal experience of *psychological* distress, as exemplified by anxiety, depression, frustration, worry, etc.
    1. Feels pretty good most of the time, very occasional dysphoria
    2. Feels anxious, depressed, and worried at times
    3. Fairly anxious and depressed; suffering a fair amount; under a good deal of pressure from within; feels *something* needs to be done about it
    4. Feels rather anxious, depressed, and worried most of the time; considerable suffering
    5. Feels under extremely great stress; extremely anxious and suffering constantly

17. Degree of impairment
    The degree to which the psychic stress or symptomatology impairs the person's ability to work, love, and play
    1. No interference or virtually no interference with work and life in general
    2. Some interference, but on the whole functions rather well
    3. Emotional difficulties definitely interfere with effective satisfying living; can't pursue duties too well but functions after a fashion
    4. Quite incapacitated but not completely so; almost constant interference of emotional problems
    5. Completely or almost completely incapacitated

18. Patient's motivation for therapy
    Willingness to participate in psychological treatment
    1. Very reluctant or resistant to therapy; virtually refuses therapy
    2. Willing to give therapy a try, but not very eager
    3. Desires psychotherapy even though he may have some reservations

4. Definitely wants psychotherapy; ready and eager to work on emotional problems

5. Very eager for psychotherapy; very anxious for psycho-therapeutic help

19. Degree of improvement expected (prognosis)

Amount of positive change expected in present psychological disturbance

1. Virtually no change in current picture expected

2. Some change expected, but not much

3. Prospects for therapy look reasonably good; definite change for the better expected

4. Rather good outlook for change; a great deal of change expected

5. "Ideal" prospects; complete alleviation of presenting problems expected

20. Degree of symptomatic improvement

This item is the outcome rating for Item 19; that is, here the observed alleviation of presenting problems and symptoms is assessed

1. Little change from inception of therapy; about same as before; essentially unchanged

2. Slight changes; symptoms somewhat improved

3. Symptoms appreciably alleviated; much less "sick," but there are still problems

4. Symptoms very markedly improved; only slight difficulties persist

5. Complete alleviation of presenting problems or symptoms

21. Over-all success of therapy

An over-all estimate of the current status which presumably resulted from therapeutic intervention, including change in subjective discomfort (Item 16), degree of impairment (Item 17), and symptom relief (Item 20), along with any additional gains beyond the more specific ones already stated. This is a global outcome rating

1. Virtually no improvement; suffers about same as before; little benefit seems apparent to any of the parties concerned

2. Some change, but report is guarded, and improvement is unimpressive

3. Appreciable improvement, but some problems persist, although on the whole patient is improved
4. Marked improvement; symptoms almost completely disappeared; patient functioning much better
5. Outstanding therapeutic success; complete relief from problems that led patient to seek therapy; patient is a "different" person; constructive use of mental energies; enthusiastic comments in report

To study the reliability of the rating procedure, we each independently rated 50 clinic charts selected at random from the total sample, which represented a 20 per cent sub-sample. Unfortunately, rater 1 had left the area when the reliability study was undertaken, and it was not possible to compare systematically 50 charts that had been rated by both research assistants; consequently, their ratings had to be combined (RA 1/RA 2). Research assistant 1 rated 18 of the 50 clinic charts and research assistant 2, 32. Since RA 2 rated a larger number of cases in the total sample, the over-representation of her ratings in the reliability study appeared reasonable.

In studying these data two approaches were used. The first was to consider only the frequency distribution of scores given by each rater in order to determine the extent to which the raters agreed. The second approach was to examine the agreement of the raters on the scores given each patient. Table E-1 gives the frequency distribution for each variable and also summed over all variables. The column headed "0" denotes inability to make a rating; when the rater merely expressed uncertainty (like "3?"), the rating was treated as though a definite judgment had been expressed. After summing the frequencies for all six variables, chi square contingency tests were performed on all data and on the professionals' ratings only, and the professionals' ratings were compared with those of the research

Table E-1. Frequency Distributions on Rated Variables

Rater	0	1	2	3	4	5	χ^2	d.f.	p
Variable 16: Amount of Subjective Discomfort									
F	0	3	5	15	21	6			
L	1	5	12	15	13	4	16.12	9	>.05
S	1	0	9	14	21	5			
RA 1/RA 2	0	0	5	22	21	2			
Variable 17: Degree of Impairment									
F	0	3	12	9	10	16			
L	1	4	11	19	10	5	16.34		>.05
S	2	1	10	18	9	10			
RA 1/RA 2	0	0	8	21	14	7			
Variable 18: Patient's Motivation for Therapy									
F	0	4	11	17	18	0			
L	4	4	16	15	10	1			
S	4	2	8	24	11	1	13.93		>.05
RA 1/RA 2	0	1	14	23	12	0			
RA 1	0	0	6	7	5	0			
RA 2	0	1	8	16	7	0			
Variable 19: Degree of Improvement Expected (Prognosis)									
F	0	2	9	23	15	1			
L	11	4	16	6	13	0	45.11		<.01
S	2	0	15	20	13	0			
RA 1/RA 2	0	0	14	25	11	0			
Variable 20: Degree of Symptomatic Improvement									
F	1	13	13	6	13	4			
L	4	15	11	10	8	2	13.81		>.05
S	3	7	13	11	14	2			
RA 1/RA 2	3	8	18	12	9	0			
Variable 21: Over-All Success of Therapy									
F	1	12	10	15	11	1			
L	4	16	17	10	3	0	11.76		>.05
S	3	14	12	12	9	0			
RA 1/RA 2	2	11	14	15	8	0			
Summary									
F	2	37	60	85	88	28			
L	25	48	83	75	57	12	89.36		<.01
S	15	24	67	99	77	18			
RA 1/RA 2	5	10	73	118	75	9			

assistants. In each of the tests chi square values were very large, indicating that different raters used different standards in making the ratings.

When the same analyses were performed on the individual variables, it became clear that much of the disagreement between raters in the interpretation of the scales occurred in Variable 19 (degree of improvement expected), where all chi square values were highly significant. However, in other instances the chi square value approximated statistical significance (.05 for Variables 16 and 17—amount of subjective discomfort and degree of impairment). Some pooling of cell frequencies was necessary in all the analyses on individual variables. This fact, together with the smaller numbers involved, tended to make these tests less sensitive to differences than the over-all tests.

Table E-2 shows the six correlation coefficients for the

Table E-2. Product-Moment Correlation Coefficients and Intraclass Correlations between Ratings

Variable	F-L	F-S	L-S	Rater L-RA 1/ RA 2	F-RA 1/ RA 2	S-RA 1/ RA 2	r
16. Discomfort	.73	.51	.67	.60	.51	.57	.66
17. Impairment	.71	.89	.71	.79	.71	.81	.79
18. Motivation	.44	.54	.52	.57	.39	.36	.58
19. Improvement expected	.35	.36	.44	.51	.51	.45	.55
20. Symptomatic improvement	.84	.83	.81	.76	.81	.70	.82
21. Over-all success	.79	.82	.80	.76	.76	.82	.80

four raters, Fox, Lessler, Strupp, and the research assistants, for each of the variables under investigation. Variables 17, 20, and 21 correlated appreciably higher than the others. The results, based on pair-wise agreement between raters, are strengthened by a measure of over-all agreement, the intraclass correlation coefficient listed in the last column of the table. These differences appear to be largely attributable to incomplete information from the clinic charts.

They usually contained specific statements on degree of impairment, symptomatic improvement, an over-all success of therapy, whereas information on other variables was often spotty and was sometimes completely absent. In those cases the raters were forced to guess. The more reliably rated variables obviously are of greater value in this study than those having lower rater agreement. Fortunately, over-all success, one of the key variables, also emerged as one of the most reliable indices.

In all statistical analyses involving these variables the ratings made by the research assistants were used. Although their reliability was by no means perfect, the professional raters (the authors) disagreed with one another as well as with the research assistants, so that their assessments could hardly be considered superior. More intensive training of raters might have led to greater uniformity in the use of the scales, but a large part of the unreliability undoubtedly derived from the fragmentary nature of the original data. While the level of agreement for all items is considered reasonably satisfactory (see Table E-3), agreement at the

Table E-3. Intraclass Correlations between Ratings

Variable	r
Amount of subjective discomfort[a]	.66
Degree of impairment[a]	.79
Patient's motivation for therapy[a]	.58
Degree of improvement expected (prognosis)[a]	.55
Degree of symptomatic improvement	.82
Over-all success of therapy	.80

[a] Based on data available at first diagnostic interview.

.50 level must be regarded as only marginally useful. On the other hand, correlations in the .80 range can hardly be improved upon, given the data available.

Appendix F
Statistical Analysis

Steps in the statistical treatment of the data are presented schematically in Figure F-1, which will clarify the following discussion. In Step *1* the basic data used in the statistical treatment were gathered together. The clinic chart data were derived from information contained in the 244 charts of the patients who originally made up the total sample. Subjective data were drawn from the 122 usable completed questionnaires (see Appendix A).

SCHEMATIC STEPS IN DATA ANALYSIS

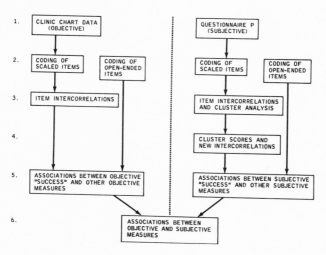

Figure F-1

In Step *2* the data were prepared for quantitative analysis. Here a distinction had to be made between information obtained from precoded and from open-ended items. Precoded items were answered on scales prepared in advance. Open-ended items were responses to questions which the patient had been invited to answer in his own words. In order to prepare these data for quantitative analysis, it was necessary to develop content codes for each item and to assign elements of the response to categories developed for this purpose.

In Step 3 item intercorrelations were made for clinic chart data and Questionnaire P data separately. Only scaled items could be used in this part of the analysis.

In dealing with the responses to Questionnaire P, we attempted to distinguish as many meaningful dimensions as possible, to study the relationships of these dimensions to one another, and, ultimately, to explore the extent to which they might relate to the clinic chart data. In this way we hoped to learn whether the patients' feelings, attitudes, and self-evaluations were wholly idiosyncratic or whether there were systematic relationships between them and the data from the clinic charts. The technique of factor analysis was not considered feasible because of the large number of items involved and the lack of independence of item responses. Instead, as in Study 1, we adopted a less rigorous approach, an informal cluster analysis (see discussion of Step 4 below).

In Step 5 the statistical relationships between the two success ratings mentioned previously and other measures from the same data source were systematically explored in order to determine which items played a part in over-all therapeutic success.

Finally, in Step 6 the "objective" clinic chart data were correlated with the "subjective" patient questionnaire data. This part of the statistical analysis was essentially an extension of Step 5.

We shall now summarize the procedures employed in analyzing the structured (precoded) items in Questionnaire P. Ten item clusters were defined and formed the basis of cluster scores. In designing Questionnaire P for Study 1, we wished to obtain, among other things, a clear picture of the manner in which the respondent viewed his psychotherapy experience. We therefore included a sizable number of items dealing with the patient's attitudes toward the therapist and the degree to which he felt respected and accepted by him, based upon the hypothesis that the "atmosphere" or "therapeutic climate" created by the therapist may play an important part in determining the course and outcome of psychotherapy. Furthermore, we wanted to find out whether most therapists took an attitude of relative detachment (on the psychoanalytic model) or established a more easy give-and-take relationship. In short, each item represented a hypothetical relationship between patient attitude and therapeutic outcome.

We also intended to measure a given attitude from slightly different vantage points. An important objective was to determine empirically whether several items could be grouped under a single heading so that these composites could be used to define and measure a given attitude area more reliably. At the same time, we anticipated that certain items—of course, we did not know which ones—would be relatively independent statistically and thus should be retained as single items. Finally, it seemed likely that there would be items whose wording was ambiguous, which provided no discrimination among respondents, or which would be unusable for other reasons. The statistical analysis, then, was intended to refine the original questionnaire and to develop a more precise and incisive instrument that might prove useful in future investigations.

The steps followed in the earlier investigation and in the present one included: (1) study of response frequencies for each item; (2) intercorrelations (Pearson r's) among all structured items; (3) systematic study of the statistical interrelationships; (4) isolation of item clusters; (5) computation of cluster scores based on items included in each composite; and (6) correlations among cluster scores, individual items, and other measures (apart from Questionnaire P).

Step 4 is the crucial stage in this process and requires further explanation. Members of the project staff, first individually and then jointly, inspected the complete table of intercorrelations. A search was then made for item pairs whose correlation was notably high, usually at the .70 to .80 level. Once such a pair was found, items which were highly correlated with both of the items in the pair were added (the correlations of the added items were usually lower). This process was continued until a point of diminishing returns was reached at which the inclusion of more items appeared "strained"; that is, the staff began to disagree on the advisability of adding them. At this juncture the correlation coefficients had usually dropped to about .50, which was generally used as a cut-off. The process was then discontinued and a new cluster started.

Thus, in constructing item clusters, although we were guided primarily by the size of the correlation coefficients, we also took into account the meaning of the items, that is, whether they seemed to belong in a given cluster. While meeting the quantitative criteria for one cluster, qualitatively an item might be more appropriate in another. The aim was to develop clusters that were internally consistent while being highly differentiated from each other. The first goal was easier to attain than the second because many of the items in Questionnaire P were at least moderately well correlated with others and consequently might be assigned to more than one cluster. The formation of clusters was partly an empirical and partly a judgmental process, and this would also have been the case, of course, if a formal factor analysis had been performed.

In Study 1 twelve clusters were isolated, composed of from two to nine items. Clusters including only two or three items obviously had to be regarded as provisional. A major reason for using the identical procedure in Study 2 was to determine whether replication on a different sample of respondents was possible. Analyses of this type are necessarily influenced by the characteristics of a particular sample and may be subject to error caused by sampling fluctuations. If replication of clusters is possible, one is clearly well advised to use them in subsequent work.

Table F-1 presents a comparison of the clusters derived independently from the two studies, as well as the item intercorrelations.* It will be noted that there is a larger degree of overlap; that is, replication was achieved in the majority of instances. Two new, albeit very tentative, clusters were defined, and several previous ones could not be replicated. The major clusters in Study 2 contained the same items as the previous ones, for the most part, although in general the number of items included in the various clusters was smaller. Clusters P1, P2, P3, P4, P5, and possibly P9 emerge as the best established—and perhaps most important —composites.

For use in subsequent statistical analyses, cluster scores were computed by simply adding up each respondent's score on every item included in a cluster. Weighting procedures seemed unnecessary for this process. The meaning of each cluster may be gleaned from the following descriptions:

Cluster P1: Therapist's Warmth (five items). This cluster appears to represent a broad estimate of the therapist's attitude during therapy, as the patient recalled it. The major dimension appeared to be warmth vs. coldness and closeness (informality) vs. distance (formality). It was, of course,

---

* There was reason to believe that patients who had had only one course of therapy (no therapy after leaving our clinic), only one therapist, and no prior or subsequent hospitalizations, as well as meeting several additional criteria, might be a "pure" group whose pattern of item correlations would yield a clearer (less contaminated) picture. We separated such patients (40) from the rest of the sample and carried out parallel analyses on both groups. Since the initial hunch was not borne out—the pattern of item correlations was virtually identical in all significant respects—we decided to use the full sample in deriving item clusters.

Table F-1. Final Clusters, Patient Questionnaire

Items		Final Cluster			

P1: Therapist's Warmth

	38	42	48	49	63
38. Therapist stiff and formal		.66 (.57)^a	−.60 (−.47)	.52 (.40)	.71 (.62)
42. Therapist cold and distant			−.73 (−.68)	.56 (.59)	.66 (.61)
48. Therapist warm				−.63 (−.70)	−.60 (−.49)
49. Therapist's tone cold					.55
63. Therapist's speech formal					(.63)

P2: Amount of Change

		18	19	73	79
18. Benefit from therapy			.86 (.91)	.72 (.78)	.55 (.57)
19. Satisfaction with therapy				.68 (.72)	.53 (.58)
73. Amount of change					.73 (.75)
79. Symptom relief					

P3: Present Adjustment—Current Status

		15	16	76	78
15. Need more therapy, ever			.67 (.66)	−.59 (−.44)	−.62 (−.71)
16. Need more therapy, now				−.72 (−.76)	−.67 (−.77)
76. Getting along now					.77 (.81)
78. Dealing with problems					

P4: Amount of Change Apparent to Others

		75a	75b	75c
75a. Change apparent to husband/wife			.73 (.80)	.62 (.77)
75b. Change apparent to close friends				.78 (.77)
75c. Change apparent to co-workers, etc.				

P5: Therapist's Interest, Integrity, and Respect

	32	33	46	47	60	61
32. Therapist respected me		.61 (.58)	−.54 (−.35)	.53 (.47)	.51 (.59)	−.28
33. Therapist interested in me			−.53 (−.47)	.70 (.66)	.66 (.75)	.58 (.61)

Table F-1. (Cont.)

46. Never sure he thought me worth while	−.56 (−.65)	−.62 (−.47)	−.43 (−.46)
47. Trusted his integrity		.50 (.59)	.52 (.66)
60. Felt accepted by him			.61 (.63)
61. No doubt of his interest			
[*P6: Not used—Uncertainty about Therapist's Feelings*]			

P7: Intensity of Emotional Experience	25	26
25. Therapy emotional experience		
26. Therapy painful experience		.53 (.50)
[*P8: Not used—Use of Technical Terms*]		

P9: Degree of Disturbance before Therapy	69	70
69. How disturbed at beginning		
70. How anxious at beginning		.55 (.66)

P10: Therapist's Experience/Activity Level [b]	24	31
24. Experience level of therapist		
31. Therapist rather active		.55 (.64)

[a] Study 1 coefficients are in parentheses.
[b] New cluster.

difficult to determine whether this represented the therapist's "true" personality or whether it referred to his behavior in therapy (i.e., his professional stance). The latter is perhaps more nearly correct.

Cluster P2: Amount of Change (four items). This cluster represents a global estimate of the degree of benefit the patient felt he derived from therapy, the extent to which he experienced change, and the degree of symptomatic improvement, as well as his over-all satisfaction with the experience. Scores based on this cluster represent the key measure of therapeutic success as experienced by the patient.

Cluster P3: Present Adjustment (four items). This composite measures how well the patient feels he is getting along now, how adequately he feels he is dealing with problems in living, and, conversely, whether he felt in need of further therapy at the time of answering the questionnaire.

Cluster P4: Amount of Change Apparent to Others (three items). The answers to the three inter-related items dealing with the amount of change apparent to husband or wife, close friends, and co-workers and acquaintances are combined here.

Cluster P5: Therapist's Interest, Integrity, and Respect (six items). This cluster measures the patient's perception of the therapist's interest, respect, and acceptance, as well as his trust in the therapist's integrity. This cluster is considered of crucial importance because the attitudes expressed here seem to permeate all other responses throughout the questionnaire.

Cluster P7:* Intensity of Emotional Experience (two items). This cluster gauges the extent to which the patient experienced psychotherapy as an intensely emotional experience in which painful feelings were mobilized.

Cluster P9: Degree of Disturbance before Therapy (two items). This cluster measures the extent to which the patient felt disturbed and anxious at the beginning of therapy. Since distress and anxiety are motivating factors for therapy, this cluster might be expected to correlate with therapeutic success.

Cluster P10: Therapist's Experience/Activity Level (two items). This cluster, not previously used, measures the extent to which the therapist was "active" in therapy, which, incidentally, was found to be correlated (.55) with his level of experience as perceived by the patient.

Most of the clusters identified in the earlier investigation emerged independently in the present one. Although the items in the various clusters were not always identical, there was a fair degree of overlap.

---

* Numbering parallels that of Study 1, which accounts for seeming inconsistencies when a cluster failed to be replicated.

Appendix G

Content Analysis of Open-Ended Items

In devising content codes for the open-ended questionnaire items, we considered it advisable to reflect as accurately as possible the patients' phenomenal descriptions of their symptoms, difficulties, and therapeutic changes instead of imposing the more common nosological schemes of psychopathology. We accepted the patients' statements largely at face value without making clinical inferences or interpreting what they were communicating. If the patient specifically mentioned a symptom or a change, it was coded. If he did not mention it, we did not code it even if there was indirect evidence that it existed.

In dealing with these responses we also kept in mind that patients might deliberately refrain from mentioning symptoms and problems they did not wish to commit to paper. Similarly, allowance had to be made for the fact that patients were writing as laymen who could not be expected to have any knowledge of psychopathology or nosological classification. The content categories which were adopted after numerous experiments were intended to be as inclusive as possible and were dictated almost totally by the material at hand. In other words, they were the product of an inductive process and embody no assumptions about systems of psychopathology, nor does the ordering of the categories have any special significance. On the other hand, we found that the range of patient responses was rather completely represented in the final categories.

The following items were considered of major importance and elicited the most exhaustive responses: Item 66: "What were your major complaints (symptoms) that led you to enter therapy, i.e., how did you view your problem(s) at the beginning of therapy?" and Item 74: "Describe the most important changes you have experienced." Responses to Item 74 were supplemented by responses to Item 20, which followed a question about the patient's satisfaction with his therapy. Item 20 asked the reason for the responses to the preceding item, which was to be answered by a check mark. Where additional material was given in Item 20, it was coded jointly with Item 74, to which it appeared closely related. The content categories are given below, and the frequencies are presented in Figure G-1.

Item 66 *

1. Sexual problems: function; behavior; thoughts
2. Physical symptoms: tired, weak, drowsy; blurred vision; heart palpitation; headaches; stomach difficulties; breathing difficulty, chest pains; dizziness; other specific physical symptoms; "physically ill," not otherwise specified; psychosomatic illness
3. Generalized anxiety (exclusive of physical symptoms): nervousness, tension, "afraid"
4. Interpersonal difficulties (specifically mentioned):
   a. problems caused by other people's actions (parents, spouse, children, boss)
   b. problems caused by feelings of others toward patient (rejection, persecution resentment, jealousy, suspicions)
   c. problems due to patient's feelings about others (anger, resentment, hostility, distrust, fear of aggression)
   d. lack of interpersonal closeness (no friends, loneliness, lack of depth)
   e. unhappy marriage
   f. other
5. Negative self-evaluation: inferiority, inadequacy; no self-confidence, unsure; insecurity; doubts about worth or self-respect
6. Loss of interest
   a. general discomfort (puzzlement, dissatisfaction with life, malaise); loss of drive (no purpose, generalized indecision, apathy); general withdrawal
   b. inability to meet life's demands and responsibilities
7. Overwhelmed (strong adjectives used): extreme despair; problems formidable; no will to live

---

* Since the frequencies in certain categories were small, a number of them were combined into the broader categories which appear in the figures.

8. External cause: "unhappy childhood or past"; loss of loved one
9. Depression (expressly stated or as mood swings)
10. Suicide (thoughts or attempts)
11. Phobias and fears
12. Guilt
13. Delusions (confusion, disorganization)
14. Concentration problems: mental blocks; inattention
15. Poor judgment and/or reality testing
16. Obsessive-compulsive symptoms: rumination; worry
17. Fantasy problems: daydreaming; nightmares; hallucinations
18. Work problems: unable to study or complete assigned work; difficulty in career decision; unable to hold job
19. Behavior problems: impulsiveness; shoplifting; alcoholism, etc.
20. Attitude toward therapy
    a. patient recognized need for therapy
    b. therapy not initiated by patient
21. Psychosis (expressly stated by patient)
22. Compulsions and rituals
23. Unclassifiable

Item 77 only
24. Status of symptoms
    a. Problems worse
    b. Problems unchanged
    c. Problems somewhat better
    d. Problems much improved
    e. No problems
25. Sense of mastery (ability to cope)
26. Problems in consciousness: amnesias; fugues; dissociations

Item 74
1. Improvement of sexual problems
2. Improvement of physical symptoms
3. Less nervousness, tension, fear
4. Improvement in interpersonal relations:
    a. recognition that problems are not "caused" by other people
    b.–c. decrease in anger, hostility, resentment, jealousy, suspiciousness; smoother interpersonal relationships; better handling of anger, aggression, etc.

   d. greater interpersonal closeness; less loneliness; greater
      depth; more pleasure in closeness
   e. improvement in marital relationship
   f. other
5. More positive self-evaluation and self-image: greater adequacy; greater independence; less sense of inferiority;
   greater self-confidence; greater security; greater sense of
   worth; greater self-acceptance
6. a. Greater zest for living; greater happiness, satisfaction;
      more purposefulness; greater decisiveness; more drive, en-
      ergy
   b. Greater ability to meet life's demands and responsibilities
7. Less hopelessness, futility
8. Improvements due to external factors
9. Less depression
10. Fewer suicidal thoughts
11. Decrease in phobias and focalized fears
12. Less guilt
13. Lessening of confusion, disorganization, delusions
14. Lessening of mental blocks and of problems surrounding
    concentration and attention
15. Improved judgment and/or reality testing: more realistic
    about one's limitations and in general; acceptance of life as
    it is; greater objectivity about goals
16. Fewer obsessions and ruminations; less worrying
17. Fewer fantasy problems; less daydreaming; fewer night-
    mares; fewer hallucinations
18. Greater productivity in work: improved ability to make
    career decisions and plan vocational goals
19. Fewer behavior problems: less impulsiveness, shoplifting,
    alcoholism, etc.
20. Attitude toward therapy:
    a. still room for improvement; could use more therapy
    b. basic rejection of therapy experience
[21. Omit]
22. Fewer compulsions and rituals
23. Unclassifiable
24. Status of symptoms (general):
    a. worse (change for the worse)
    b. unchanged
    c. problems somewhat less

  d. problems much less
  e. no problems; tremendous change
25. Increased sense of mastery and ability to cope
26. Increased insight into feelings and motives; better understanding of self

COMPARISON OF PRESENTING SYMPTOMS FROM
PATIENT DESCRIPTIONS AND CLINIC CHARTS

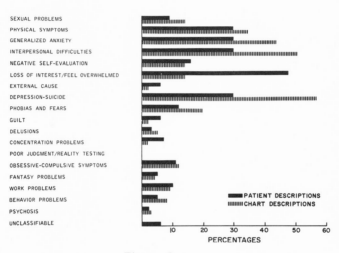

Figure G-1

It will be seen that the codes for Items 66 and 74 are complementary: if a patient complained of sexual problems under Item 66 and noted an improvement in that area under Item 74, he received a score in this category under both items. Among the advantages of this system is that it permits a direct comparison between original symptoms and improvements. Codings for the various items were, of course, performed independently, in the sense that all responses to a given item were coded consecutively without reference to other item responses. The categorizations were performed jointly by the authors, and differences of opinion were resolved through group discussion. Most disagreements resulted from the ambiguous wording of the patients' responses. In each instance, a response was given as many codes as appeared necessary to reflect its content. Thus some patients received only one code, while others received as many as seven.* In summary, it may be said that we found the system highly satisfactory. It included almost every pertinent comment or statement a patient might make.

Responses to Item 81 ("In general, how would you describe your attitude toward the therapist?") were handled in somewhat similar fashion. Responses were coded into four major categories, categories I and II permitting parallel codings of positive and negative responses.

Item 84 ("What adjectives do you feel best describe the therapist's attitude toward you while you were in therapy?") was scored on a seven-point scale ranging from negative to positive, as follows:

Code	Description
1	Strong negative feelings
2	Generally negative
3	Mildly negative; distant
4	Natural; businesslike; doing a job
5	Mildly positive; pleasant; showed interest
6	Caring; helpful
7	Strong positive feelings

Item 81

Positive   *Negative*

I. Attitudes toward Therapist

1. Respect   6. Dependence
2. Trust and confidence   7. Gratitude and appreciation
3. Admiration   8. Lack of respect
4. Liking and friendship   9. Distrust; uncertainty; lack
5. Love and sexual feelings   of confidence

* Since some of the coding categories were used very infrequently, it became necessary to combine them with related ones in subsequent statistical analyses.

10. Fear
11. Dislike

12. Anger, contempt, hate
13. Jealous
14. Ambivalence *now*
15. Changed during therapy (includes all transient early feelings; ambivalence during course of therapy)

II. Characteristics Attributed to Therapist

20. General positive excellence; fine person
21a. Capable, intelligent, insightful
21b. Experienced
22. Understanding
23. Warm, accepting, interested, kind, patient
24. Firm
25. Neutral, impersonal, detached
26a. Friendly
26b. Caring, eager to help
27. Respectful, considerate

28. Inexperienced, novice
29. Lack of understanding
30. Cold, distant, disinterested
31. Negative physical attributes
32. Passive, weak
33. Generally negative; poor therapist

III. Patient's Feelings about the Relationship

40. Valuable relationship
41. Ease of communication
42. Relaxed, natural
43. Manipulation of relationship; lack of honest communication; eager to please
44. Stiff, uncomfortable, ill at ease, embarrassed, foolish
45. Frightened
46. Reluctant, resistant
47. Difficulty separating from therapist
48. Lack of communication
49. Gained insight

IV. Comments about Therapy and Results

51. Positive
52. Negative
59. Unclassifiable

The authors coded all responses jointly, following the same procedure as outlined for the open-ended items mentioned above. The results are given in Figure G-2.

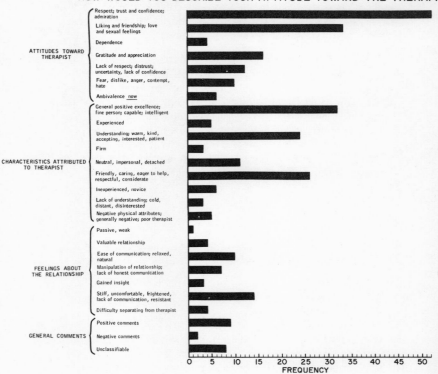

Figure G-2

Appendix H

Rated Over-All Success

vs. Selected Items from Questionnaire P

Item 13.[a] Additional Therapy after OPD

Success[b]	Yes (1)	No (2)	Total
Low	16	29	45
Medium	7	35	42
High	3	26	29
Total	26	90	116

Item 16. How Much in Need of Further Therapy Do You Feel Now?

Success	None or Slight (1–2)	Could Use More (3)	Considerable or Very Great (4–5)	Total
Low	21	12	12	45
Medium	20	13	8	41
High	23	4	2	29
Total	64	29	22	115

Item 19. How Satisfied Are You with the Results of Your Psychotherapy Experience?

Success	Dissatisfied (1–3)	Fairly–Moderately Satisfied (4–5)	Highly Satisfied (6–7)	Total
Low	8	22	15	45
Medium	5	13	23	41
High	0	6	22	28
Total	13	41	60	114

[a] This is a "synthetic" item: it consists of information which the research staff abstracted and coded from the patients' responses.

[b] Code: Low, 1–2; Medium, 3; High, 4–5. All chi squares are statistically significant beyond the .05 level.

*Item 73. How Much Do You Feel You Have Changed
as a Result of Psychotherapy?*

Success	None–Some (1–3)	Fair Amount (4)	Great Deal (5)	Total
Low	14	12	19	45
Medium	14	14	14	42
High	2	10	17	29
Total	30	36	50	116

*Item 76. How Well Do You Feel You Are
Getting Along Now?*

Success	Poorly (1–4)	Fairly Well (5)	Very Well (6–7)	Total
Low	12	19	14	45
Medium	9	21	13	43
High	1	10	16	27
Total	22	50	43	115

Appendix I

Rated Over-All Success vs.

Attitudes toward Therapist

(Questionnaire P)

Success[a]	Disagree (1–2)	Agree (4–5)	Total

Item 30. There Were Times I Experienced Intense Anger Toward My Therapist.

	Disagree (1–2)	Agree (4–5)	Total
Low	9	33	42
Medium	19	21	40
High	11	15	26
Total	39	69	108

Item 39. The Therapist's Manner Was Quite Natural and Unstudied.

Low	15	21	36
Medium	8	29	37
High	4	23	27
Total	27	73	100

Item 48. There Usually Was a Good Deal of Warmth in the Way He Talked to Me.

Low	13	22	35
Medium	6	33	39
High	5	21	26
Total	24	76	100

Item 60. I Usually Felt I Was Fully Accepted by the Therapist.

Low	10	29	39
Medium	1	37	38
High	3	23	26
Total	14	89	103

[a] Code: Low, 1–2; Medium, 3; High, 4–5. In those instances in which "Undecided" responses (3) numbered fifteen or more, separate chi squares were computed; since the results were virtually identical, the "Undecided" category has been omitted throughout. All chi squares are statistically significant beyond the .05 level.

211

Item 65. My Therapist Stressed Intellectual Understanding as Much as Emotional Experiencing.

Low	12	14	26
Medium	8	24	32
High	3	17	20
Total	23	55	78

REFERENCES

Alexander, F. 1956. *Psychoanalysis and psychotherapy: Developments in theory, technique, and training.* New York: W. W. Norton.

Alexander, F., and French, T. M. 1946. *Psychoanalytic therapy: Principles and application.* New York: Ronald Press.

Bachrach, A. J.; Erwin, W. J.; and Mohr, J. P. 1965. The control of eating behavior in an anorexic by operant conditioning techniques. In *Case studies in behavior modification,* eds. L. P. Ullmann and L. Krasner, pp. 153–63. New York: Holt, Rinehart and Winston.

Berenson, B. G., and Carkhuff, R. R., eds. 1967. *Sources of gain in counseling and psychotherapy.* New York: Holt, Rinehart and Winston.

Bergin, A. E. 1963. The effects of psychotherapy: Negative results revisited. *Journal of Counseling Psychology* 10:244–50.

Colby, K. M. 1964. Psychotherapeutic processes. *Annual Review of Psychology* 15:347–70.

Erikson, E. H. 1968. *Identity: Youth and crisis.* New York: W. W. Norton.

Eysenck, H. J. 1952. The effects of psychotherapy: An evaluation. *Journal of Consulting Psychology* 16:319–24.

————. 1959. Learning theory and behavior therapy. *Journal of Mental Science* 105:61–75.

————. 1961. The effects of psychotherapy. In *Handbook of abnormal psychology*, ed. H. J. Eysenck, pp. 697–725. New York: Basic Books.

Fingarette, H. 1963. *The self in transformation.* New York: Basic Books.

Frank, J. D. 1959. Problems of control in psychotherapy as exemplified by the psychotherapy research project of the Phipps Psychiatric Clinic. In *Research in psychotherapy*, eds. E. A. Rubinstein and M. B. Parloff, pp. 10–26. Washington, D.C.: American Psychological Association.

————. 1961. *Persuasion and healing.* Baltimore: Johns Hopkins Press.

Frank, J. D., et al. 1963. Immediate and long-term symptomatic course of psychiatric outpatients. *American Journal of Psychiatry* 120:429–39.

Freud, S. 1950. Analysis terminable and interminable. In *Collected papers*, ed. Ernest Jones, 5:316–57. 5 vols. London: Hogarth Press.

Fromm-Reichmann, F. 1950. *Principles of intensive psychotherapy.* Chicago: University of Chicago Press.

————. 1954. Psychoanalytic and general dynamic conceptions of theory and of therapy. *Journal of the American Psychoanalytic Association* 2:718.

Gill, M. M. 1954. Psychoanalysis and exploratory psychotherapy. *Journal of the American Psychoanalytic Association* 2:771–97.

Goldstein, A. P., Heller, K., and Sechrest, L. B. 1966. *Psychotherapy and the psychology of behavior change.* New York: Wiley.

Hollingshead, A. B., and Redlich, F. C. 1958. *Social class and mental illness.* New York: Wiley.

Knight, K. P. 1941. Evaluation of the results of psychoanalytic therapy. *American Journal of Psychiatry* 98:434–46.

Lang, P. J., and Lazovik, A. D. 1963. Experimental desensitization of a phobia. *Journal of Abnormal and Social Psychology* 66:519–25.

Luborsky, L. 1962. The patient's personality and psychotherapeutic change. In *Research in psychotherapy*, eds. H. H.
Strupp and Luborsky, 2:115–33. Washington, D.C.: American Psychological Association.

Matarazzo, J. D. 1965. Psychotherapeutic processes. *Annual
Review of Psychology* 16:181–224.

Menninger, K. 1958. *Theory of psychoanalytic technique.* New
York: Basic Books.

Paul, G. L. 1966. *Insight vs. desensitization in psychotherapy.*
Stanford, Calif.: Stanford University Press.

Pfeffer, A. Z. 1959. A procedure for the evaluation of the results of psychoanalysis. *Journal of the American Psychoanalytic Association* 7:418–45.

————. 1961. Follow-up study of a successful analysis. *Journal
of the American Psychoanalytic Association* 9:698–718.

————. 1963. The meaning of the analyst after analysis. *Journal of the American Psychoanalytic Association* 11:229–44.

Pfouts, J., Wallach, M. S., and Jenkins, J. W. 1963. An outcome study of referrals to a psychiatric clinic. *Social
Work* 8:79–86.

Rogers, C. R., and Dymond, R. F. 1954. *Psychotherapy and
personality change.* Chicago: University of Chicago Press.

Rogers, C. R., et al. 1967. *The therapeutic relationship and its
impact: A study of psychotherapy with schizophrenics.*
Madison Wis.: University of Wisconsin Press.

Rubinstein, E. A., and Parloff, M. B., eds. 1959. *Research in
psychotherapy.* Vol. 1. Washington, D.C.: American Psychological Association.

Schjelderup, H. 1955. Lasting effects of psychoanalytic treatment. *Psychiatry* 18:109–33.

Schofield, W. 1964. *Psychotherapy: The purchase of friendship.* Englewood Cliffs, N.J.: Prentice-Hall.

Shlien, J. M., et al., eds. 1968. *Research in psychotherapy.*
Vol. 3. Washington, D.C.: American Psychological Association.

Strupp, H. H. 1963. Psychotherapy revisited: The problem of
outcome. *Psychotherapy* 1:1–3.

Strupp, H. H., and Luborsky, L., eds. 1962. *Research in psy-*

chotherapy. Vol. 2. Washington, D.C.: American Psychological Association.

Strupp, H. H.; Wallach, M. S.; and Wogan, M. 1964. Psychotherapy experience in retrospect: Questionnaire survey of former patients and their therapists. *Psychological Monographs* 78.

Sullivan, H. S. 1953. *The interpersonal theory of psychiatry*. New York: W. W. Norton.

Szasz, T. S. 1961. *The myth of mental illness: Foundations of a theory of personal conduct*. New York: Hoeber.

———. 1965. *The ethics of psychoanalysis: The theory and method of autonomous psychotherapy*. New York: Basic Books.

———. 1967. Behavior therapy and psychoanalysis. *Medical Opinion and Review* (June), pp. 24–29.

Tarachow, S. 1963. *An introduction to psychotherapy*. New York: International Universities Press.

Truax, C. B., and Carkhuff, R. R. 1967. *Toward effective counseling and psychotherapy; training and practice*. Chicago: Aldine.

Wallerstein, R. S. 1968. The psychotherapy research project of the Menninger Foundation: A semi-final view. In *Research in psychotherapy*, ed. J. M. Shlien et al., 3:584–605. Washington, D.C.: American Psychological Association.

Wolpe, J. 1958. *Psychotherapy by reciprocal inhibition*. Stanford, Calif.: Stanford University Press.

Wolpe, J., and Lazarus, A. A. 1966. *Behavior therapy techniques*. New York: Pergamon.

INDEX